TIMELINE 2000

Does God Have a Plan For Mankind?

NEW EVIDENCE!

JAMES MICHAEL HILE

WinePress Publishing
MUKILTEO, WA 98275

© 1998 James Michael Hile. All rights reserved

Printed in the United States of America

Cover design by James Michael Hile
Layout by Mike Tibbit

Packaged by WinePress Publishing, PO Box 1406, Mukilteo, WA 98275. The views expressed or implied in this work do not necessarily reflect those of WinePress Publishing. Ultimate design, content, and editorial accuracy of this work is the responsibility of the author(s).

No part of this publication may be reproduced, stored in a retrieval system or transmitted in any way by any means, electronic, mechanical, photocopy, recording or otherwise, without the prior written permission of the copyright holder, except for brief quotations in printed reviews.

Unless otherwise noted, Scripture quotations in this book are taken from the King James Version of the Bible.

ISBN 1-57921-079-1
Library of Congress Catalog Card Number: 97-62314

── *Dedication* ──

This book is dedicated to:

GOD ALMIGHTY
The ultimate source of all knowledge and wisdom and the author of eternal salvation to all who believe

My mother and father who set the example

The many radio and television ministers who feed me daily

Libraries

The author wishes to express appreciation to the following institutions and libraries for use of their reference and research material.

ARKANSAS- Arkadelphia: Henderson State University, Huie Library; Ouachita Baptist University, Riley-Hickingbotham Library
Cabot: Arlene Cherry Memorial Library; First Baptist Church Library
Conway: Central Baptist College, J.E. Cobb Library; Hendrix College (Methodist); University of Central Arkansas
Fayetteville: University of Arkansas at Fayetteville; University Baptist Church Library, J. Sidlow Baxter Library
Fort Smith: Fort Smith Public Library
Hot Springs: Garland County Library
Jacksonville: Esther Dewitt Nixon Public Library
Jonesboro: Arkansas State University
Little Rock: Arkansas State Library; Church of Christ Library, Sixth and Izard; Little Rock Public Library; Missionary Baptist Seminary, C.N. Glover Library; Philander Smith College Library; University of Arkansas at Little Rock, Ottenheimer Library
North Little Rock: William F. Laman Public Library
Pine Bluff: University of Arkansas at Pine Bluff, John B. Watson Memorial Library
Russellville: Arkansas Tech University, Tomlinson Library
Searcy: Harding University, Brackett Library (Church of Christ)

CALIFORNIA- Berkeley: Graduate Theological Union, The Flora Lamson Hewlett Library; Member Schools: American Baptist Seminary of the West; The Church Divinity School of the Pacific (Episcopal); Dominican School of Philosophy and Theology; Franciscan School of Theology; The Jesuit School of Theology at Berkeley; Pacific Lutheran Theological Seminary; Pacific School of Religion (Multi-denominational);

Libraries

San Francisco Theological Seminary (Presbyterian); Starr King School for the Ministry (Unitarian Universalist)
San Francisco: San Francisco Public Library

DISTRICT OF COLUMBIA- Washington, D.C.: George Washington University; Library of Congress

FLORIDA- Fort Lauderdale: Knox Theological Seminary (Presbyterian)
Jacksonville: Jacksonville Public Library, Main Library

GEORGIA- Atlanta/Woodstock: Cobb County Library

ILLINOIS- Chicago: Chicago Public Library, Moody Bible Institute The University of Chicago Library, The Joseph Regenstein Library
Wheaton: Wheaton College, Wheaton College Library (Presbyterian)

LOUISIANA- New Orleans: Loyola University Library (Catholic) Tulane University, Howard-Tilton Memorial Library

MAINE- Portland: Portland Public Library

MISSOURI- Kansas City: St. Paul School of Theology, Dana Dawson Library (Methodist)
Saint Louis: Aquinas Institute of Theology (Catholic) Saint Louis University, Pius XII Memorial Library, Divinity Library, Doisy Library (Catholic) Saint Louis Public Library, Barr Branch; Washington University, Olin Library
Springfield: Assemblies of God Theological Seminary, Cordas C. Burnett Library

OKLAHOMA- Oklahoma City/Bethany: Southern Nazarene University, R. L. Williams Learning Resource Center

PENNSYLVANIA- Pittsburgh: University of Pittsburgh, Hillman Library

TENNESSEE- Memphis: Christian Brothers University, The Plough

Library, (Catholic); Memphis Public Library, Goodwin Institute Library, Cossitt Library; Memphis Shelby County Public Library; Mid America Baptist Theological Seminary, Ora Byram Allison Library; The University of Memphis
Nashville: Tennessee State University, Brown-Daniel Library, Avon Williams Campus Library

TEXAS- Austin: The Episcopal Theological Seminary of the Southwest; University of Texas at Austin, Perry Castanada Library
Dallas: Dallas Theological Seminary, Turpin Library, Mosher Library
Fort Worth: Southwestern Baptist Theological Seminary, A. Webb Roberts Library
Houston: Houston Graduate School of Theology; Houston Public Library, Central Library; Rice University, Fondren Library

WEST VIRGINIA- Charleston: Kanawha County Public Library

Acknowledgments

Over the past eight years as the research and writing of *Timeline 2000* took place, several people were helpful in moving the project towards completion. My brother, Robert, assisted in the design of the timeline charts while brother Winston and sister Lynda reviewed the manuscript for errors.

A big thank you is extended to my close friend, Cliff Ellis, for his review and critique, as well as Scott Williams, a successful businessman in Little Rock. Dr. John Lewis and Pastor Don and Maggie Chandler also reviewed the manuscript and offered comments.

Many thanks is accorded to my new friend, William T. "Terry" James who has authored and edited several books on Bible prophecy. Terry offered helpful advice and referred me to his editor and indispensable assistant, Angie Peters. Angie provided the professional editing and timely review necessary to speed up the publication of *Timeline 2000*.

The encouragement, support and extraordinary patience provided by my wife Joyce, daughters, Monica and Kristel, and sons, Brent and Jordan, contributed substantially in the completion of this project. The writing of *Timeline 2000* was a difficult and complex task that had to be worked in between a demanding full-time business career and family responsibilities.

Although my plans were to have published *Timeline 2000* several years ago, unavoidable delays prevented this from happening. Hopefully, these delays resulted in a better manuscript that will ultimately bring more honor and glory to our Lord and Saviour Jesus Christ!

Contents

	Preface	11
	Introduction	13
1.	Can I Trust the Bible?	15
2.	Why Read the Bible?	23
3.	God Is in Control!	29
4.	The Bible: Gateway to the Past	45
5.	The Bible and Old Testament Events	55
6.	Does History Really Repeat Itself?	65
7.	The Three Returns of Israel	79
8.	Israel: God's Prophetic Clock!	85
9.	The Time of the End: Have We Arrived?	97
10.	Signs of the Times: Where Is Our Society Heading?	105
11.	What Is Your Spiritual Temperature?	119
12.	The Great Escape!	127

Preface

If you are skeptical, curious, or perhaps an adherent to the truths contained in the Bible, *Timeline 2000* will challenge you to evaluate your spiritual condition and discover God's plan for your life. God is in control! God has a specific plan for your life! God wants you to accept His plan of salvation so that you will be assured of a spiritually fulfilled life on this earth with the added assurance that a place has been reserved for you in heaven. Until you find God's plan for your life, there will always be an emptiness that cannot be filled by anyone or anything this world has to offer.

The author is keenly aware of the many attempts in recent years to assign dates for future events foretold in the Bible. Some may attempt to label these writings as such. *Timeline 2000*, however, does not make any predictions concerning the future and does not set any dates for future events. Although the content of the book includes the years leading up to the year 2000 A.D., the author does not suggest or imply that specific prophetic events described in the Bible will happen immediately before or after the year 2000. Only God knows the future! *"Known unto God are all his works from the beginning of the world"* (Acts 15:18).

The historical dates and resulting time cycles that are presented in *Timeline 2000* give a brief but revealing picture of the past 4,000 years, which includes the current century in which we are living. The author believes world events in the light of Bible prophecy are on "Fast Forward," and the evidence is overwhelming that we are living in the time period described by the prophet Daniel as "the time of the end." The author also believes that many who are living today are witnessing the events leading up to the return of Jesus Christ to planet earth.

As we continue our journey into one of the most spiritually exciting times since Jesus Christ came to the earth almost 2000 years ago, those who love God should focus on the truths that are contained in the scriptures in order to be able to discern between truth and error

Timeline 2000

and right and wrong. In a world where deception and lying are becoming commonplace, we are reminded of the freedom that comes from knowing the truth. Jesus Christ told His disciples nearly 2000 years ago: "*...If ye continue in my word, then are ye my disciples indeed; And ye shall know the truth, and the truth shall make you free*" (John 8:31,32).

Introduction

"God that made the world and all things therein, seeing that he is Lord of heaven and earth...hath determined the times before appointed and the bounds of their habitation." Acts 17: 24, 26b

Many believe that dates for Old Testament events are too vague and uncertain to be reliable. Although that remains the case for many of the early events described in the Bible, the dates for events from the time of Abraham, Isaac and Jacob (Israel) (c. 2000 B.C.), in many cases, have been reliably established during this century.

Late one evening, during the first week of January 1990, I was scanning through a book at the downtown Little Rock Public Library. *The Bible Almanac,* by Packer, Tenney and White (Thomas Nelson), featured an extensive section on Bible chronology that caught my interest. A survey of the subject matter, "Bible Chronology -Finding the Dates of Bible Events," revealed that many of the dates for events in the Bible that scholars were previously unable to accurately determine have now been confirmed.

Interest sparked from these initial findings led me on an extensive investigative journey that resulted in research at many theological, educational and governmental institutions throughout the country.

My premise: If major historical dates, such as the date of the Exodus, could be pinpointed accurately, we would have concrete reference points for God's dealings with His chosen people, Israel. Since God has a plan for Israel, the dates when He has intervened in Israel's affairs might be part of a master plan, like links on a chain, that extend down through the corridor of time and into the 20th century.

My pursuit of this premise resulted in some amazing discoveries that clearly and unmistakably show God's dealings with Abraham, Isaac, Jacob and the Nation of Israel from around 2000 B.C. to the present time in which we are living, the last decade of the 20th century.

Timeline 2000

From 2000 B.C. to 2000 A.D., God has been openly and mysteriously carrying out His plan of redemption for mankind. Thus, the title, *Timeline 2000*, seems to appropriately describe the past 4000 years that have transpired and reflects the exciting times in which we are living. Unmistakable signs of our times are pointing to the soon return of Jesus Christ to planet earth. May God be glorified through these new discoveries!

— 1 —

CAN I TRUST THE BIBLE?

"It is impossible to rightly govern the world without God and the Bible." [1]

—George Washington

"The Book of Books has been our most faithful and instructive guide, and has implanted in our hearts universal redemption. If we continue to walk in its light, both the nation and its leaders will be successful." [2]

—David Ben-Gurion

"I believe the Bible is the best gift God has ever given to man. All the good from the Saviour of the world is communicated to us through this book." [3]

—Abraham Lincoln

The Uniqueness of the Bible

The Bible is the greatest book ever written. Contained within its pages are answers to the four most important questions concerning man's existence here on planet earth: *Who am I? Where did I come from? Why am I here?* and *Where am I going when I die?* Questions concerning the creation of the universe, the glories of heaven, the horrors

Timeline 2000

of hell and God's redemptive plan for mankind are all dealt with in God's Holy Word.

Dr. Charles C. Ryrie, professor of systematic theology at Dallas Theological Seminary, points out the uniqueness of the Bible:

> "...The Bible claims to come from the true God, to reveal the true condition of mankind and to reveal the way to be acceptable to God. It offers hope, not the despair that characterizes other sacred writings." [4]

The Bible, God's written revelation to man, tells us about the original sin of Adam and Eve and how mankind became separated from God. The central theme is the salvation of man through faith in Jesus Christ. The Bible contains 66 books written by over 40 authors on three continents in three different languages over a 1500-year span that covers over 40 generations. The authors, who were from all walks of life, included kings and princes, poets and philosophers, prophets and statesmen, fishermen and scholars. [5,6]

> "Does God have a plan which includes the earth and the human race? If so, can man know it? The answer is an emphatic, Yes! God does have a plan, and that plan is clearly outlined in the Bible from Genesis to Revelation. Man can know God's plan clearly if only he will come to the Bible and submit his mind and heart to the ministry of the Holy Spirit." [7]
>
> Dr. Lehman Strauss

From the first chapter of Genesis to the last chapter of the Book of Revelation, the Bible contains all the essential information we need to understand God's plan for our lives. Our responsibilities to God as His creation and God's commitment to us when we choose to follow His precepts and teachings are all contained within the pages of the Book of Books, the Bible.

Cecil B. DeMille (1881-1959), an American movie producer who directed the legendary movie *The Ten Commandments*, stated: "After more than sixty years of almost daily reading of the Bible, I never fail to find it always new and marvelously in tune with the changing needs of every day." [8]

The Bible contains the one and only plan that has been approved by God that will assure us of eternal life in heaven. God wants us to accept His plan for our lives and enjoy the benefits and rewards that He has reserved for us in this life and the life to come. Obedience to God's plan should be our top priority!

The Inspiration of the Scriptures

The Divine inspiration of the scriptures has been a cornerstone doctrine of the Christian faith for many centuries. The word "inspire" means "to influence, move, or guide by divine or supernatural inspiration." [9] Inspiration implies that God is the Author of the Scriptures, and that God's Word can be relied upon as an accurate and reliable source of information for making decisions and providing guidance in this life.

Charles H. Spurgeon (1834-1892), a famous English preacher of the nineteenth century, remarked: "If I did not believe in the infallibility of Scripture—the absolute infallibility of it from cover to cover, I would never enter this pulpit again!" [10]

The apostle Paul, who once persecuted Christians, later became a zealous proponent of the Christian faith. In one of his letters to Timothy, Paul wrote:

> *"All scripture is given by inspiration of God and is profitable for doctrine, for reproof, for correction, for instruction in righteousness: That the man of God may be perfect, throughly furnished unto all good works"* (II Timothy 3:16,17).

Theologians throughout the centuries have defined and redefined the doctrine of the inspiration of the Scriptures. B. B. Warfield, a reformed theologian, made the following classic statement concerning the inspiration of the Bible:

> "The doctrine of plenary inspiration holds that the original documents of the Bible were written by men, who, though permitted to exercise of their own personalities and literary talents, yet wrote under the control and guidance of the Spirit of God, the result being in every word of the original documents a perfect and errorless recording of the exact message which God desired to give to man." [11]

The unfailing truths contained in the Holy Scriptures testify to the guiding hand of God in preserving His Word. Another classic statement of the inspiration of the scriptures reads:

> "We believe the Holy Bible was written by men divinely inspired, and is a perfect treasure of heavenly instruction; that it has God for its author, salvation for its end, and truth without any mixture of error for its matter; that it reveals the principles by which God will judge us; and therefore is, and shall remain to the end of the world, the true center of Christian union, and the supreme standard by which all human conduct, creeds, and opinions shall be tried." [12]

As a testimony to the unique nature and inspiration of the Scriptures, William F. Albright, considered to be one of the greatest archaeologists of all times, concluded:

> "The Bible towers in content above all earlier religious literature; and it towers just as impressively over all subsequent literature in the direct simplicity of its message and …its appeal to men of all lands and times." [13]

The Reliability of God's Word

How reliable is the Bible? Can I depend upon it? Can I trust it to guide me through the many problems and trials that I will face in this life? Robert E. Lee, commander of Confederate forces in the Civil War, said: "In all my perplexities and distresses, the Bible has never failed to give me light and strength." [14]

The old expression "experience is the best teacher" may or may not be the best way to learn; however, its effectiveness cannot be denied. A prudent person learns from his mistakes in life; however, a wise person not only learns from his own mistakes, he learns from the mistakes and success of others.

William E. Gladstone (1809-98), Prime Minister under Queen Victoria, stated:

> "I have known ninety-five of the world's great men in my time, and of these, eighty-seven were followers of the Bible.

The Bible is stamped with a 'Specialty of Origin', and an immeasurable distance separates it from all competitors." [15]

To be successful in our journey through this life, we should learn from and pattern our lives after those who have already found the "key to success." The "key to success" in this life and the life to come is obedience to God. For many, God's Word has been a faithful guide and companion and a source of knowledge and wisdom for making sound decisions.

Dr. Henry Morris, president of the Institute for Creation Research in El Cajon, California, points out:

> "The greatest scientists of all time—those who have laid the foundations of discovery and investigation that have contributed the most to all that is really worthwhile in our modern civilization—have in most cases been sincere, humble Christians who believed in the Bible as the literally inspired Word of God." [16]

At the top of the list is Sir Isaac Newton, acknowledged by many to be the greatest man of science who ever lived. Morris also points out other high-powered names in the field of physics, biology and medicine: Lord Kelvin, Clerk Maxwell, Louis Pasteur and Lord Lister.

In astronomy, famous names include Galileo, Kepler, Copernicus and, in modern times, Sir William and Sir John Herschel were all Bible-believing scientists. Morris relates that Pascal, Faraday, Ramsay, Pupin, Dana, Linnaeus, Agassiz, Dawson, and a long list of others could be added as well.

The Accuracy of the Scriptures

Are the Scriptures in the Bible accurate? Many who have sought to discredit the Bible's teachings in times past have had their claims disproved as new evidence became available. A commonly held belief, even by some professing Christians, is that the Bible contains much scientific error. Sir William Herschel (1738-1822), an English astronomer who made many discoveries, including the planet Uranus, and who mapped numerous galactic nebulae, concluded: "All human discoveries seem to be made only for the purpose of confirming more and more strongly the truths contained in the Sacred Scriptures." [17]

Archaeology also confirms the accuracy of the Bible. For example, Nelson Glueck, the renowned Jewish archaeologist, has said that "…no archaeological discovery has ever controverted a biblical reference." [18] William F. Albright, the dean of American archaeologists, stated: "We may rest assured that the consonantal text of the Hebrew Bible…has been preserved with an accuracy perhaps unparalleled in any other Near Eastern literature." [19]

Dr. Henry Morris concludes: "…There exists today not one unquestioned find of archaeology that proves the Bible to be in error at any point. Truly this book is the Word of God!" [20]

Those who are skeptical of the Bible many times change their opinion when they approach it with an open mind and look objectively at its contents. Josh McDowell, a traveling representative of Campus Crusade for Christ who has been introducing skeptics to Jesus Christ for several decades, relates his experience:

> "There was a time in my life when I myself tried to shatter the historicity and validity of the Scriptures. But I have come to the conclusion that they are historically trustworthy. If a person discards the Bible as unreliable in this sense, then he or she must discard almost all the literature of antiquity." [21]

The Perseverance of the Bible

No other book in history has been subjected to as much criticism as the Bible. Although the skeptics and critics have come and gone, the Book of books is alive and well! Bernard Ramm, in his book *Protestant Christian Evidences*, states:

> "A thousand times over, the death knell of the Bible has been sounded, the funeral procession formed, the inscription cut on the tombstone, and committal read. But somehow the corpse never stays put. No other book has been so chopped, knived, sifted, scrutinized, and vilified. What book on philosophy or religion or psychology… of classical or modern times has been subject to such a mass attack as the Bible? With such venom and skepticism? With such thoroughness and erudition? Upon every chapter, line, and

tenet? The Bible is still loved by millions, read by millions, and studied by millions." [22]

The leader of the Protestant reformation, Martin Luther, remarked: "It is a miracle how God has so long preserved his Book! How great and glorious it is to have the Word of God!" [23] Theologian H.L. Hastings presents another powerful testimony to the endurance of God's Word:

"Infidels for eighteen hundred years have been refuting and overthrowing this book, and yet it stands today as solid as a rock. Its circulation increases, and it is more loved and cherished and read today than ever before. Infidels with all their assaults, make about as much impression on this book as a man with a tack hammer would on the Pyramids of Egypt. When the French monarch proposed the persecution of the Christians in his dominion, an old statesmen and warrior said to him, 'Sire, the Church of God is an anvil that has worn out many hammers.' So the hammers of infidels have been pecking away at this book for ages, but the hammers are worn out, and the anvil still endures. If this book had not been the book of God, men would have destroyed it long ago. Emperors and popes, kings and priests, princes and rulers have all tried their hand at it; they die and the book still lives."[24]

The Bible testifies to the permanent nature of the Scriptures and the temporary status that is accorded to the things of this world:

"The grass withers, the flower fades, but the word of God stands forever" (Isaiah 40:8).
"For all flesh is as grass, and all the glory of man as the flower of grass. The grass withereth, and the flower thereof falleth away: But the word of the Lord endureth for ever" (I Peter 1:24, 25).
"Heaven and earth shall pass away, but my words shall not pass away" (Matthew 24: 35).

Can we trust the Bible? Many of the world's most famous and successful leaders in government, science, medicine and other walks of life have put their trust in the Holy Scriptures.

Timeline 2000

The truths of God's Word provide comfort, protection, direction and security in this life and the life to come.

> *"Come unto me, all ye that labour and are heavy laden, and I will give you rest. Take my yoke upon you, and learn of me; for I am meek and lowly in heart: and ye shall find rest unto your souls. For my yoke is easy, and my burden is light"* (Matthew 11:28-30).

— 2 —

WHY READ THE BIBLE?

"I want to know one thing, the way to heaven…God himself has condescended to teach the way…He hath written it down in a book. Oh, give me that book! At any price give me the book of God!" [1]

—John Wesley

"Without a knowledge of the Bible, a knowledge of ourselves, our origin, our spirit-our destiny and our future is impossible." [2]

—David Ben-Gurion

"The Bible that is falling apart usually belongs to someone who isn't." [3]

—Vance Havner

A Blueprint for Daily Living

Before a building is constructed, there needs to be a plan that describes how the foundation, walls and roof will be built. This plan, called a blueprint, determines the quality, durability and longevity of the structure. In like manner, every person needs a plan or blueprint for his life. Dr. Tim LaHaye, a nationally recognized speaker on family life issues, states: "Daily Bible reading is to your spiritual life what daily eating is to your physical life." [4]

The wise person builds his life on a solid foundation that leads to eternal life, whereas the foolish person builds his life on an unstable foundation that leads to death and destruction. In the Sermon on the Mount, Jesus described these two types of foundations:

> *"Enter ye in at the strait gate: for wide is the gate, and broad is the way, that leadeth to destruction, and many there be which go in thereat: Because strait is the gate, and narrow is the way, which leadeth unto life, and few there be that find it…Not every one that saith unto me, Lord, Lord, shall enter into the kingdom of heaven; but he that doeth the will of my Father which is in heaven…*
>
> *Therefore whosoever heareth these sayings of mine, and doeth them, I will liken him unto a wise man, which built his house upon a rock: And the rain descended, and the floods came, and the winds blew, and beat upon that house; and it fell not: for it was founded upon a rock.*
>
> *And every one that heareth these sayings of mine, and doeth them not, shall be likened unto a foolish man, which built his house upon the sand: And the rain descended, and the floods came, and the winds blew, and beat upon that house; and it fell: and great was the fall of it"* (Matthew 7: 13-27).

A Road Map to Heaven

In order to clearly see "the big picture" and understand "the Master's blueprint" for eternal life, we must read the Bible regularly. J. H. Bernard stated: "Salvation, the salvation of man, is the final purpose of the whole Bible." [5] Those who read the Bible and follow its instructions will build a life that is stable. A firm foundation built upon godly principles will help us endure the storms of this life and will assure that a place has been reserved for us in heaven when death comes knocking at our door.

Although the books of the Bible were written a long time ago, the teachings contained within its pages apply to the times in which we live. John Brown once said: "The doctrines of the Bible are all practical and its laws all reasonable." [6] Adhering to Biblical principles will keep us on the right path. John Bunyan, author of the classic *Pilgrim's Progress,* remarked: "Sin will keep you from this book, or this book will keep you from sin." [7]

We must not only be "hearers" of the Word, as instructed in James 1:22; we must also be "doers" of the Word. D.L. Moody, a famous preacher of the nineteenth century, said: "The Scriptures were not given to increase our knowledge but to change our lives." [8]

As faithful "doers" of the Word, our top priority should be to make sure our relationship with God is in order. We should not postpone the most important decision we will ever make in our life. For many people, tomorrow will never come. The prophet Isaiah implores us to seek the Lord now:

> *"Seek ye the Lord while he may be found, call ye upon him while he is near: Let the wicked forsake his way, and the unrighteous man his thoughts: and let him return unto the Lord, and he will have mercy upon him; and to our God, for he will abundantly pardon. For my thoughts are not your thoughts, neither are your ways my ways, saith the Lord. For as the heavens are higher than the earth, so are my ways higher than your ways, and my thoughts than your thoughts"* (Isaiah 55:6-9).

Why Study Bible Prophecy?

> "Bible Prophecy proves beyond any reasonable doubt that God knows and controls the future. He's not sitting on the circle of the earth as a mere observer, He is in charge!" [9]
>
> John Hagee

The prophetic Scriptures occupy a large portion of the Word of God. In fact, in both the Old and New Testaments, whole books are devoted to the subject of prophecy.

> "About one-fourth of the Bible was predictive when it was written, and obviously divine revelation is intended to alert us of future events with the intent of preparing believers for the events before they happen. Prophecy was never intended to be a contentious subject for people to argue over, but rather a practical subject to alert people to prepare for God's future

plan. Much has been lost by misunderstanding and neglect of the prophetic Scriptures." [10]

> Dr. John F. Walvoord

If God devoted so much space to the subject, then it must be important. We should certainly not neglect its study, either ignorantly or through a willfully defiant attitude. The Lord commands us to watch and be prepared!

Those who seriously teach God's Word would certainly not tear the prophetic scriptures out of the Bible and throw them away. Unfortunately, that very thing is effectively accomplished when the prophetic teachings contained in the Bible are ignored.

> "There are many people today who have relegated the prophetic scriptures to oblivion. They feel that a man has to be either mentally unbalanced, a religious fanatic, or a heretic in doctrine to manifest interest in the study of prophecy. This is particularly true among men who profess to love the Word of God but who have no respect for the authority and integrity of the scriptures." [11]
>
> Dr. J. Dwight Pentecost

Dwight L. Moody stated: "If God did not mean to have us study the prophecies, He would not have put them into the Bible. Some of them are fulfilled, and He is fulfilling the rest, so that if we do not see them all completed in this life, we shall in the world to come. Prophecy, as has been said, is the mould in which history is cast." [12]

Originally published in 1878, William E. Blackstone's classic work *Jesus Is Coming*, which has been distributed in over 40 foreign languages with over a million copies in print, cautions us that we should not reject the prophetic teachings in the Bible because of false teachings or misapplication of the prophetic Scriptures.

> "It may be you disapprove the study of prophecy, because Jesus said: '*But of that day and hour knoweth no man*' (Matthew 24:36), and, '*It is not for you to know the times or the seasons which the Father hath put in his own power*' (Acts 1:7). Dear reader! Do not conceive that the study of prophecy consists

merely in the setting of dates or forecasting future events. For wise reasons the Master has withheld from us *'the day and the hour'* when He will come, but He called the Pharisees hypocrites, because they could not discern the signs of the times, and He has commanded us to WATCH, and He has pronounced a blessing upon the study of prophecy (Revelation 1:3)." [13]

Bible Prophecy: Key to Understanding the Future!

In the latter part of the Olivet Discourse, Christ described some of the conditions that would exist in the world just before His return. Immoral conditions as in *"the days of Noah"* prior to the flood and *"the days of Lot"* prior to the destruction of Sodom and Gomorrah will be prevalent.

> *"And as it was in the days of Noah, so shall it be also in the days of the Son of man. They did eat, they drank, they married wives, they were given in marriage, until the day that Noah entered into the ark, and the flood came, and destroyed them all. Likewise also as it was in the days of Lot; they did eat, they drank, they bought, they sold, they planted, they builded; But the same day that Lot went out of Sodom it rained fire and brimstone from heaven, and destroyed them all. Even thus shall it be in the day when the Son of man is revealed"* (Luke 17:26-30).

The prophet Daniel was told that at the time of the end *"the wicked shall do wickedly: and none of the wicked shall understand; but the wise shall understand"* (12:10). The spiritually wise person, living during the time preceding Christ's return, will compare the prophetic Scriptures with current world events in order to understand and perceive God's program as it begins to unfold.

> "God rules. He is sovereign. He is the One who changes the times and the epochs, who removes and establishes kings. Because He is Alpha and Omega, the beginning and the end, He knows the beginning from the end; therefore, if you want to know what the future holds, you need to seek the wisdom of the One who holds the future in His hands." [14]
>
> Kay Arthur

Timeline 2000

At Christ's First Coming, Jesus confronted the religious leaders of the day (Scribes and Pharisees) because they could not *"...discern the signs of the times..."* (Matthew 16:1-4). Concerning Christ's Second Coming, those who are serious about God's Word should not be found guilty of repeating the fateful mistakes made by the Scribes and Pharisees. May God grant each person reading this message the wisdom to study and understand the times in which we are living!

3

GOD IS IN CONTROL!

"Remember the former things of old: for I am God, and there is none else; I am God, and there is none like me, Declaring the end from the beginning, and from ancient times the things that are not yet done, saying, My counsel shall stand, and I will do all my pleasure:"

—Isaiah 46:9-11

"Thus saith the Lord, thy redeemer, and he that formed thee from the womb, I am the Lord that maketh all things; that stretcheth forth the heavens alone; that spreadeth abroad the earth by myself;"

—Isaiah 44:24

"Hast thou not known? hast thou not heard, that the everlasting God, the Lord, the Creator of the ends of the earth, fainteth not, neither is weary? There is no searching of his understanding."

—Isaiah 40:28

Has your life ever seemed to be out of control? Have outside events and circumstances influenced some or many of the decisions you have made in your life? We may have control over some of the decisions in our lives; however, much of our destiny depends upon when we were born, where we were born, to whom we were born, and other external factors that are beyond our control. We grow old, suffer from health problems and eventually die. God is not subject to these limitations: *"Behold, I am the Lord, the God of all flesh: Is there anything too hard for me?"* (Jeremiah 32:27).

THE SOVEREIGN GOD OF THE UNIVERSE

What does it mean when we say that God is sovereign? A simple answer would be: God is in control!

> *"The Lord of hosts hath sworn, saying Surely as I have thought, so shall it come to pass; and as I have purposed, so shall it stand:"* (Isaiah 14:24).

God's sovereignty, however, is far greater than anything we can imagine. Unlike the many created things that exist on earth and in the universe, God was not created and, therefore, has no beginning. He has always existed and will always exist: *"I am Alpha and Omega, the beginning and the ending, saith the Lord, which is, and which was, and which is to come, the Almighty"* (Revelation 1:8).

God is in complete control of the past, the present and the future. He is omnipotent (all powerful), omniscient (all knowing), and omnipresent (present everywhere). There is no limit to God's power, knowledge or understanding.

> *"Thus saith the Lord the King of Israel, and his redeemer the Lord of hosts; I am the first, and I am the last; and beside me there is no God...Who hath measured the waters in the hollow of his hand, and meted out heaven with the span, and comprehended the dust of the earth in a measure, and weighed the mountains in scales, and the hills in a balance?...Who hath wrought and done it, calling the generations from the beginning?...Behold, the former things are come to pass, and new things do I declare: before they spring forth I tell you of them...before me there was no God formed, neither shall there be*

after me. I, even I, am the Lord; and beside me there is no saviour" (Isaiah 44:6, 40:12, 41:4, 42:9, 43:10,11).

The Heavens Reveal God's Glory

The Bible is very clear concerning God's existence and His creation. God's plan for mankind is also clearly explained in the pages of His Word:

"The heavens declare the glory of God; and the firmament sheweth his handy-work" (Psalms 19:1).

God is the Almighty Creator of the Universe. His wisdom and power brought forth all living things that exist on the earth, and all things are sustained by His mighty hand.

"He hath made the earth by his power, he hath established the world by his wisdom, and hath stretched out the heavens by his discretion. When he uttereth his voice, there is a multitude of waters in the heavens, and he causeth the vapours to ascend from the ends of the earth; he maketh lightnings with the rain, and bringeth forth the wind out of his treasures" (Jeremiah 10:12,13).

The Divine Watchmaker

An eighteenth-century British theologian-naturalist, William Paley, put forth a simple but concrete story called "The Watchmaker Argument" which has proved to be one of the most compelling arguments for the existence of God.

"In crossing a heath, suppose I pitched my foot against a stone, and were asked how the stone came to be there; I might possibly answer, that, for anything I knew to the contrary, it lain there for ever: nor would it perhaps be very easy to show the absurdity of this answer. But suppose I had found a watch upon the ground, and it should be inquired how the watch happened to be in that place; I should hardly think of the answer which I had before given, that for anything I knew, the watch might have always been there…The watch must have had a maker: that there must have existed, at some time, and at some place or other, an artificer or artificers, who formed it for the purpose which we find it actually to answer; who comprehended its construction, and designed its use....Every indication of contrivance, every manifestation of design, which existed in the watch, exists in the works of nature; with the difference, on the side of nature, of being greater or more, and that in a degree which exceeds all computation." [1]

"No one of sound mind, Paley explains, would ever conclude that a watch was the product of bits of dust, dirt, and rock being shuffled together under natural processes. Even if the natural processes were allowed to operate for a very long time, there would still be no rational hope for a watch to be assembled. Yet, as all the naturalists of Paley's day admitted and all the biologists of today emphatically concur, the complexity and capability of living organisms far transcends anything we see in a watch. If a watch's complexity and capability demand an intelligent and creative maker, surely," Paley reasoned, "the living organisms on our planet demand a Maker of far greater intelligence and creative ability." [2]

No other planet in the observable universe is like the earth. Scientific evidence shows beyond a reasonable doubt that life on earth could not have developed without Divine assistance. Someone remarked that for life to spontaneously develop on the earth without Divine intervention would be a far greater miracle than having a tornado pass through a junkyard and promptly assemble a Boeing 747 jet from the rubbish. Those who deny the existence or intervention of God in the creation process must in effect have greater faith than that which is necessary to believe and trust in God.

The Bible's viewpoint concerning those who refuse to acknowledge God is straightforward: *"The fool hath said in his heart, There is no God"* (Psalms 14:1). Those who choose not to accept or acknowledge God's existence as Creator lack proper discernment and discretion. God, however, is patient and forgiving towards anyone who will turn from their ways and follow Him.

"Come now, and let us reason together, saith the Lord: though your sins be as scarlet, they shall be as white as snow;

though they be red like crimson, they shall be as wool. If ye be willing and obedient, ye shall eat the good of the land: But if ye refuse and rebel, ye shall be devoured with the sword: for the mouth of the Lord hath spoken it" (Isaiah 1:18-20).

The Sustainer

God is not only the Creator of all things, He also sustains and upholds His creation and creatures that inhabit the earth. In His infinite love for mankind, He makes special provision for those who seek Him and keep His commandments.

"He giveth power to the faint; and to them that have no might he increaseth strength. Even the youths shall faint and be weary, and the young men shall utterly fall: But they that wait upon the Lord shall renew their strength; they shall mount up with wings as eagles; they shall run, and not be weary; and they shall walk, and not faint" (Isaiah 40:29-31).

God's protection and wisdom is available to those who call upon Him and seek His guidance. If God is for you, who will be able to stand and prevail against you?

"For thus saith the high and lofty One that inhabiteth eternity, whose name is Holy; I dwell in the high and holy place, with him also that is of a contrite and humble spirit, to revive the spirit of the humble, and to revive the heart of the contrite ones" (Isaiah 57:15).

Our Judge

Because of God's holy and righteous nature, He does not tolerate sin. God chooses, in some cases, to postpone the judgment of man's sin; however, a complete accounting of every man's transgressions will one day be given. Those who trust in their riches rather than God's mercy and grace make a big mistake!

"Be not thou afraid when one is made rich, when the glory of his house is increased; For when he dieth he shall carry nothing away: his glory shall not descend after him. Though while he lived

> *he blessed his soul: and men will praise thee, when thou doest well to thyself. He shall go to the generation of his fathers; they shall never see light...the wicked shall perish, and the enemies of the Lord shall be as the fat of lambs: they shall consume; into smoke shall they consume away...Behold, these are the ungodly, who prosper in the world; they increase in riches...Surely thou didst set them in slippery places: thou castedst them down into destruction. How are they brought into desolation, as in a moment! they are utterly consumed with terrors. As a dream when one awaketh...Now consider this, ye that forget God, lest I tear you in pieces, and there be none to deliver"* (Psalm 49:16-19, 37:20, 73:12, 18-20, 50:22).

Some choose to ignore the Scriptures concerning God's judgment; however, God takes His Word seriously, and we should do the same. Everyone's deeds, whether bad or good, will one day be judged by a Holy and Righteous God. *"...Because he hath appointed a day, in the which he will judge the world in righteousness"* (Acts 17:31).

Evil men have done horrible and cruel things to each other during both periods of war and times of peace. The mental and physical torture that has been carried out by depraved men defies description. Punishments inflicted by men on each other, however, do not come close to the torture and terror that awaits those who reject God's plan of salvation. God tells us that the horrors of hell are much worse than anything man can do to you while on earth.

> *"...fear not them which kill the body, but are not able to kill the soul: but rather fear him which is able to destroy both soul and body in hell"* (Matthew 10:28).

Those who take God's warnings lightly will be in for a big surprise when the Lord returns to judge those who have rejected Him!

> *"Behold, the Lord cometh with ten thousands of His saints, to execute judgment upon all, and to convince all that are ungodly among them of all their ungodly deeds which they have ungodly committed, and of all their hard speeches which ungodly sinners have spoken against Him"* (Jude 14,15).

"The Son of man shall send forth his angels, and they shall gather out of his kingdom all things that offend, and them which do iniquity; And shall cast them into a furnace of fire: there shall be wailing and gnashing of teeth" (Matthew 13:41,42).

Our Redeemer

God wants us to turn to Him and trust Him for our salvation. Adam and Eve's transgression in the Garden of Eden condemned the human race. Because of God's love and forgiving nature, however, He has provided a way to redeem mankind.

"I, even I, am he that blotteth out thy transgressions for mine own sake, and will not remember thy sins" (Isaiah 43:25).

Anyone willing to turn from his ways and accept God's forgiveness can have access to God's blessings here on earth and be assured of eternal life in heaven.

"The Lord is not slack concerning his promise, as some men count slackness; but is longsuffering to us-ward, not willing that any should perish, but that all should come to repentance" (II Peter 3:9).

Those who have put their faith and trust in their knowledge, wealth, authority, possessions or other temporary things this world has to offer have not exercised good judgment. God's priorities for us are totally different from what the world expects of us.

"Thus saith the Lord, Let not the wise man glory in his wisdom, neither let the mighty man glory in his might, let not the rich man glory in his riches: But let him that glorieth glory in this, that he understandeth and knoweth me, that I am the Lord which exercise loving-kindness, judgment, and righteousness, in the earth: for in these things I delight, saith the Lord" (Jeremiah 9:23,24).

If you have not trusted in Jesus Christ as your personal Saviour, God does not hear your prayers. Proverbs tells us: *"The Lord is far from the wicked: but he heareth the prayer of the righteous"* (15:29).

God's wisdom seems foolish to those who are preoccupied with and consumed by the things this world has to offer. Worldly wisdom offers many pleasures and temporary rewards for a brief period of time. Spiritual wisdom, however, offers eternal rewards. God tells us to shun worldly wisdom and become fools as far as the world is concerned in order that we might become spiritually wise and choose God's plan that leads to eternal life rather than the world's plan that leads to eternal death.

> *"Let no man deceive himself. If any man among you seemeth to be wise in this world, let him become a fool, that he may be wise. For the wisdom of this world is foolishness with God... And again, The Lord knoweth the thoughts of the wise, that they are vain. Therefore let no man glory in men"* (I Corinthians 3:18-21).

Our Friend

> *"A man that hath friends must shew himself friendly: and there is a friend that sticketh closer than a brother"* (Proverbs 18:24).

Everyone needs at least one good and faithful friend. Our friends on earth are important; however, God offers a permanent friendship that will not fail us as earthly friends sometime do. Is God your friend? If we accept God's plan of salvation and put our trust in Him, He will always be there when we need him.

> *"...I will never leave thee, nor forsake thee"* (Hebrews 13:5).
> *"The name of the Lord is a strong tower: the righteous runneth into it, and is safe"* (Proverbs 18:10).
> *"God is our refuge and strength, a very present help in trouble"* (Psalm 46:1).

God wants us to have faith in His ability to guide us. Since He knows everything about the past, present and future, He knows what path our lives should take.

> *"Trust in the Lord with all thine heart; and lean not unto thine own understanding. In all thy ways acknowledge him, and he shall direct thy paths. Be not wise in thine own eyes: fear the Lord, and depart from evil"* (Proverbs 3: 5-7).

> *"Trust in the Lord, and do good…Delight thyself also in the Lord; and he shall give thee the desires of thine heart. Commit thy way unto the Lord; trust also in him; and he shall bring it to pass"* (Psalms 37:3-5).

People who are self-centered and full of pride forfeit God's blessings. Those who fear the Lord, however, open up God's storehouse of treasures. God protects those who fear Him and keep His commandments!

> *"I sought the Lord, and he heard me, and delivered me from all my fears…The angel of the Lord encampeth round about them that fear him, and delivereth them. O taste and see that the Lord is good: blessed is the man that trusteth in him. O fear the Lord, ye his saints: for there is no want to them that fear him.*
>
> *The righteous cry, and the Lord heareth, and delivereth them out of all their troubles. The Lord is nigh unto them that are of a broken heart; and saveth such as be of a contrite spirit. Many are the afflictions of the righteous: but the Lord delivereth him out of them all…The Lord redeemeth the soul of his servants: and none of them that trust in him shall be desolate"* (Psalms 34:4-22).

The Lord's protection from the forces of evil that operate in this world allows us to help accomplish His plan of redemption for mankind before we exit this planet and head to our permanent home in heaven.

> *"Lay not up for yourselves treasures upon earth, where moth and rust doth corrupt, and where thieves break through and steal: But lay up for yourselves treasures in heaven, where neither moth nor rust doth corrupt, and where thieves do not break through nor steal: For where your treasure is, there will your heart be also"* (Matthew 6: 19-21).

If God is not already your friend, make Him your friend today! His guidance, counsel and protection will be available to you in both the good times and bad times.

> *"Seek ye the Lord while he may be found, call ye upon him while he is near: Let the wicked forsake his way, and the unrighteous man his thoughts: and let him return unto the Lord, and he*

Timeline 2000

will have mercy upon him; and to our God, for he will abundantly pardon" (Isaiah 55:6,7).

TIME, THE TWENTIETH CENTURY, AND THE COMPUTER

Time! What is it? How do we measure time? Saint Augustine (354-430), a Roman monk, asked: "What, then, is time? If no one asks me, I know what it is. If I wish to explain it to him who asks me, I do not know."

Time is sometimes represented as a flowing stream that has no beginning and no end. The expression, "time marches on!" implies that time cannot be stopped, speeded up or slowed down. In fact, the time-related word chronology comes from the classical Greek word chronos, which "signifies time viewed as a flowing stream—a stream that cannot be stopped, but can be measured." [3]

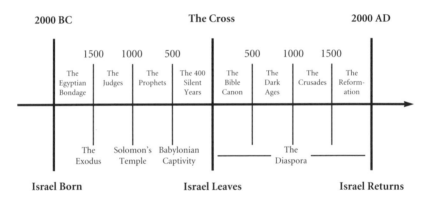

The Bible exhorts us to redeem the time and use it wisely (Ephesians 5:15-17) and compares life to a vapour that is here for a brief period of time before vanishing away (James 4:13-15).

The Great Solar Clock

The rotation period of the earth around the sun provides a reference point that helps us keep track of time. The precision with which the earth has circled the sun for thousands of years is a testimony to God's sovereignty and protection over this planet. Discoveries during the 20th century in the field of astronomy have given us a greater understanding of how the solar system and the universe operate. Astronomers can determine the exact hour, day and year of past, present and future

God is in Control!

solar and lunar eclipses by using the seemingly limitless resources of the computer.

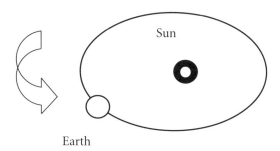

Earth

The orbit of the earth around the sun can be likened to a huge clock that keeps precise time. The sun represents the center of the clock face. Ninety three million miles (92,960,000) away from the sun is the earth, which represents the outer circumference of this great solar clock. Every 365 1/4 days, the year hand, represented by the earth, completes its circuit in the heavenlies. [4]

The Precision of God's Universe

What a marvelous timepiece God has created! The earth travels at a speed of 18.46 miles per second (66,456 m.p.h.) Mathematical calculations reveal that the earth returns to its same relative location each year with less than a fraction of a second deviation after traveling over one half billion miles (582,553,296) around the sun. No wonder the psalmist declared:

> *"The heavens declare the glory of God; and the firmament sheweth his handywork...In them hath he set a tabernacle for the sun, which is as a bridegroom coming out of his chamber, and rejoiceth as a strong man to run a race. His going forth is from the end of the heaven, and his circuit unto the ends of it: and there is nothing hid from the heat thereof"* (Psalm 19:1-6).
>
> *"The sun also ariseth, and the sun goeth down, and hasteth to his place where he arose"* (Ecclesiastes 1:5).
>
> *"He appointed the moon for seasons: the sun knoweth his going down"* (Psalms 104:19).

The extrabiblical Book of Enoch (I Enoch), which is quoted in the Book of Jude (14,15), acknowledges the precision with which God's luminaries complete their assigned periods.

> "All who are in the heavens know the work. They know that the heavenly luminaries change not their paths; that each rises and sets regularly, every one at its proper period, without transgressing the commands which they have received...They behold the earth, and understand what is there transacted from the beginning to the end of it. They see that every work of God is invariable in the period of its appearance...Again they consider the days of summer that the sun is upon it at its very beginning... That the works at the beginning of every existing year, that all his works, are subservient to him, and invariable; yet as God has appointed, so are all things brought to pass."[5]

Astronomy and the Bible

Since the orbits of the sun, moon and earth do not vary substantially, we can determine the dates of many of the solar and lunar eclipses recorded by ancient historians. Comparison of the dates of these astronomical sightings with historical writings and archaeological findings helps us pinpoint the exact dates of many ancient events.[6]

At least nine eclipses occurring between the years 763 B.C. and 491 B.C. establish the chronology of the ancient Near East.[7] By using these absolute reference points, we can reconstruct other events mentioned in the Bible and secular history that occurred before or after the absolute date.

The Babylonians, Egyptians and Astronomy

Ancient astronomers recorded many celestial events that have proved crucial to establishing reliable historical dates. For example, geographer and astronomer Ptolemy accurately recorded and dated the years of Babylonia's rulers from 747 B.C. down to the second Christian century. Ptolemy also recorded and dated more than eighty astronomical events such as eclipses of the moon on March 17, 721 B.C. and July 16, 523 B.C.[8]

God is in Control!

The Assyrians, Israel and Astronomy

The Assyrians, located northeast of modern day Israel between the Tigris and Euphrates Rivers, like the Egyptians, were keenly interested in the science of astronomy. Israel's strategic location between Assyria, Babylon and Egypt allowed events that were happening in Israel over 2500 years ago to be dated with the help of modern day discoveries in the fields of archaeology and astronomy.

"The Assyrians based their history on the data of astronomy, and so we can check the Assyrian dates against the movements of the stars, which our present knowledge enables us to plot accurately. Then we can use that information to pinpoint the dates of Old Testament events."

For example: "The Assyrian record says that an eclipse of the sun occurred in the month of Simanu during Bur-Sagale's term of office. Astronomers tell us that the eclipse occurred on June 15, 763 B.C. Therefore, Bur-Sagale governed in 763 B.C., and we can use this date to establish the dates of other Assyrian leaders." [9]

The Time of Christ's Birth

Chronologists have tried to determine the time of Jesus Christ's birth by using the Bible, astronomy and ancient historical sources such as the writings of Josephus. As a small child, Jesus was taken into Egypt by Joseph and Mary to escape Herod the Great's decree to slay all male children under age two. Herod died shortly thereafter, and an angel of the Lord appeared in a dream to Joseph and told him to take the young child and his mother and return to Israel.

Josephus' writings state that prior to Herod's death there was an eclipse of the moon. According to astronomical calculations, eclipses were visible in Palestine on March 23 and September 15, 5 B.C.; March 12, 4 B.C.; and January 9, 1 B.C. Shortly after one of these lunar eclipses, Herod put his son, Antipater, to death, and five days later he died. Soon after Herod's death, the Passover was near at hand. Herod's death is believed to have been between March 29 and April 4, 4 B.C. The passover in 4 B.C. fell on April 11 (Nisan 14). [10] Dates given for Christ's birth generally range from 8 B.C. to 1 B.C., with 6 B.C. to 4 B.C. being the most prevalent. [11]

Does God Have a Time Schedule?

Does God have a time schedule that is logical and predetermined, yet hidden until some future date, or are we left totally in the dark concerning the timing of God's future plan for this earth? God, who inhabits eternity, is not subject to the constraining influences of time; however, He does intervene in the affairs of this world in order to carry out His sovereign plan for mankind.

During the Old Testament times, Amos, the prophet, stated: *"Surely the Lord God will do nothing but he revealeth his secret unto his servants the prophets"* (3:7). It was in the fullness of time that God sent forth His Son to redeem mankind, who was under the curse of the law (Galations 4:4). When the hour of Christ's sacrifice for our sins arrived, He was delivered by the determinate counsel and foreknowledge of God into wicked hands to be crucified (Acts 2:23). After three days, Christ was raised up by God and showed himself alive by many infallible proofs for forty days (Acts 1:3) before ascending into heaven where he now makes intercession for us (Hebrews 7:25).

Historically, God has revealed His plans to His chosen people, the children of Israel. The timing of God's revelation to His people has been, in many cases, just prior to its fulfillment. At other times, many years or centuries passed before a prophecy was fulfilled.

In order to understand the course of future events on God's timetable, we should keep our eye on the nation of Israel, the city of Jerusalem and those nations that are involved in the Mideast peace process.

Daniel the prophet was told that the prophecy given to him was sealed and could not be understood until the time of the end (12:4,9) and *"at the time appointed the end shall be."* (8:19) As revealed in the Scriptures, God definitely has a time schedule! In order to understand what God will do in the future, it is important to know how and when He has acted in the past. An in-depth study of Bible history and Bible prophecy is therefore highly relevant to the times in which we are living. Edwin R. Thiele (1895-1986), who served as Professor of Antiquity at Andrews University, summed up the importance of chronology and history in understanding the Bible:

> "Chronology is important. Without chronology it is not possible to understand history, for chronology is the backbone of history. We know that God regards chronology as important,

for He has put so much of it into His Word. We find chronology not only in the historical books of the Bible, but also in the prophetic books, in the Gospels, and in the writings of Paul…If we would understand the Bible, we must strive to understand its chronology, for from the opening of Genesis to the close of Revelation the Bible deals with time." [12]

— 4 —

THE BIBLE

Gateway to the Past

"CHRONOLOGY IS THE BACKBONE OF HISTORY... Without exact chronology, there can be no exact history...For more than two thousand years, Hebrew chronology has been a serious problem for Old Testament scholars. Every effort to weave the chronological data of the kings of Israel and Judah into some sort of harmonious scheme seemed doomed to failure...The mysterious numbers of the kings must at length be made to reveal their secrets...The establishment of the correct chronology of a nation is always a matter of some importance, and in the case of the Hebrews—in view of the important role they have played in world events throughout the ages—this is particularly true." [1]

—Edwin R. Thiele

Have you ever wanted to know more about your ancestors? Where did they come from? How did they make a living? What kind of problems did they experience? What historical events (military, economic, social or religious) forced them to move to another land in order to survive?

The answer to these questions and many others relies on an accurate and reliable source of historical information. Determining the dates and history of significant events in the past can help us find solutions to many of the perplexing problems we face in the world today. This chapter presents an established, reliable dating system for Old Testament events that has been accepted and followed by many Bible scholars during the last half of this century.

Determining Accurate Bible Dates

In order to answer the why, when, where and how questions of history, we must find a way to reconstruct the past. Reconstructing man's past is an ongoing process that depends upon ancient historical documents, archaeological discoveries, astronomy and, to a large extent, on historical events described in the Old Testament.

> "Until a correct chronology of a nation has been established, the events of that nation cannot be correctly integrated into the events of neighboring states. If history is to be a true and exact science, then it is of fundamental importance to construct a sound chronological framework about which may be fitted the events of states and the international world." [2]
>
> Edwin R. Thiele

Within the field of Bible chronology, experts try to establish "absolute dates" which are reasonably certain, as they are based upon reliable, accurate data.

A Reliable Dating System Begins to Emerge

During the twentieth century, and more specifically during the last half of this century, there has been a growing consensus among some conservative Bible scholars concerning critical dates of Old Testament events. Some of the major disagreements in dates given by liberal scholars arise from different methods of interpreting the Old Testament Scriptures.

Those who believe the Bible's method of recording time should be taken literally are contrasted by those who do not believe the Scriptures should be accepted at face value, but should be molded to fit previously conceived dating schemes that have been derived from arbitrary dating methods.

Around the midpoint of the twentieth century, a dating system was proposed that offered solutions to many of the problems that had baffled Old Testament chronologists in the past. Edwin Richard Thiele

The Bible: Gateway to the Past

(1895-1986), a professor of biblical studies at Andrews University, Barrien Springs, Michigan, completed an in-depth study of the dating methods used by Judah and Israel from the division of Solomon's kingdom to the fall of Jerusalem (c. 900-600 B.C.), a period covering over 300 years.

Professor Thiele's chronology placed the division of the Hebrew Kingdom at 931/930 B.C. after King Solomon died. Dr. Thiele, whose research was the basis for his doctoral dissertation at the Oriental Institute of the University of Chicago, introduced his initial study of the chronology of the Hebrew kings to students of the Bible and the ancient Near Eastern world.

In July 1944, Thiele's writings were published in the *Journal of Near Eastern Studies* under the title of "The Chronology of the Kings of Judah and Israel."[3,4] The material was later published by the University of Chicago Press under the title *The Mysterious Numbers of the Hebrew Kings* in 1951, by Eerdmans in 1965 and by Zondervan in 1983.

Thirty Years Later

In April of 1982, Dr. Thiele's preface to a third edition of his writings stated:

> "Thirty years after the publication of my solution to the problem of the mysterious numbers of the Hebrew kings comes a need for a new edition. Confused and erroneous though these numbers appeared to be, they have proven themselves to be remarkably accurate… It is my hope that this presentation will serve to bring confidence in the biblical numbers of the Hebrew kings, in the God who placed them on their thrones, and in the principles of righteousness He expected them to uphold. This confidence, now so woefully lacking, is our primary need in our troubled and perplexed times. If we would restore confidence in God, we must restore confidence in the Bible—confidence that comes through an intelligent trust."[5]
>
> Edwin R. Thiele
April, 1982

Fifty Years Later

In 1994, fifty years after the original release, Kregel Publications offered a new edition by special arrangement with Zondervan Publishing House. Dr. Thiele's chronology of the Kings of Judah and

Israel has remarkably withstood the test of time and is regarded by many as the authority on the subject.

Thiele's writings have been accepted by many academic institutions and scholars around the world. For example, Dr. Eugene H. Merrill, Professor of Semitics and Old Testament studies at Dallas Theological Seminary, stated in his book, *Kingdom of Priests:* "We are accepting as our basic starting point Thiele's authoritative reconstruction of the chronology of the divided monarchy." [6]

Gleason Archer, professor of Old Testament at Trinity Divinity School, Deerfield, Illinois, remarked in his review of the 1965 edition of Thiele's book:

> "When this study of the chronology of the Divided Kingdom of Israel was first published in 1951 by this outstanding Seventh-Day Adventist scholar, it was almost immediately recognized to be the most adequate treatment of the subject yet produced. One proof of its wide acceptance is the frequency with which it is referred to by writers of varied persuasion, both liberal and conservative. Another is the fact that a second, revised edition has been published to meet the continuing demand of the public. The revision was so minor, incidentally, that the author himself makes no mention of it in his introduction. He says only, 'No evidence has been forthcoming that has given me cause to change my views on any item of major importance.'" [7]

Thiele's chronology has maintained its position in the academic world for more than fifty years. The authoritative *Cambridge Ancient History* publication adopted Thiele's chronology, which placed Solomon's death at 931 B.C. A representative of Paternoster Press in Britain called Dr. Thiele's work "the basis of all subsequent investigation in this field, and the standard authority on the subject." [8] For additional study of the subject matter and other dating methods, refer to Appendix A, B, C, and the references. [9]

The discovery of the ancient Hebrews' dating methods by Dr. Thiele has helped resolve many of the dates of Old Testament events. The dates of these events, along with other established historic dates, form the basis for the timeline chart located on the back cover and at the end of chapter eight. Before the timeline chart can be developed, however, certain key dates must be established.

Determining the Date of Solomon's Temple

The period of the Kings of Israel began with Saul, who was the first King of Israel. Saul was followed by David, who was succeeded by Solomon, David's son by Bathsheba. After Solomon's death, the kingdom of Israel was divided, with Jeroboam leading the northern kingdom of Israel and Rehoboam leading the southern kingdom of Judah.

THE KINGDOM OF ISRAEL

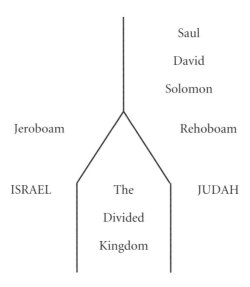

A DOOR TO THE PAST
From King Solomon to the Divided Kingdom

Evidence from the Bible, archaeology and Thiele's chronology have helped scholars establish the years of Solomon's reign. [10] We know, based upon I Kings 11:42-43, that Solomon reigned for forty years:

> *"And the time that Solomon reigned in Jerusalem over all Israel was forty years. And Solomon slept with his fathers, and was buried in the city of David his father: and Rehoboam his son reigned in his stead."*

According to Dr. Thiele's chronology, Jeroboam and Rehoboam began their reigns in 931/930 B.C. following the death of King Solomon. [11] Solomon's forty-year reign must have begun in 971-970 B.C.

Timeline 2000

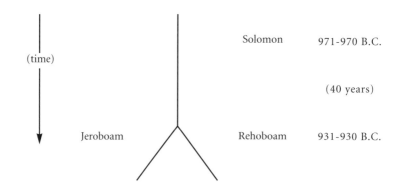

A BRIDGE TO THE PAST
Solomon's Temple and the Exodus from Egypt

Since the reigns of King David and King Saul were, like Solomon's, forty years, knowing the dates of Solomon's reign allows us to establish the dates of Saul (c. 1050-1010 B.C.) and David's reign (c. 1010-970 B.C.) (II Samuel 5:4, I Kings 2:11, Acts 13:21).

If the date of Solomon's reign opens a door to the past, I Kings contains an even more amazing historical link, or bridge, to the past.

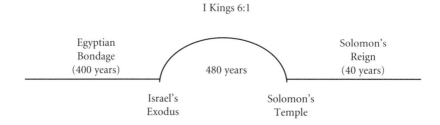

The Scripture passage around which many of the critical dates of the Old Testament pivot is found in I Kings 6:1. This passage links the time Moses lived to the time of Solomon, a 480-year span.

> "And it came to pass in the four hundred and eightieth year after the children of Israel were come out of the land of Egypt, in the fourth year of Solomon's reign over Israel, in the month Zif, which is the second month, that he began to build the house of the Lord" (I Kings 6:1).

> "In the fourth year was the foundation of the house laid, in the month Zif: And in the eleventh year, in the month Bul, which

is the eighth month, was the house finished throughout all the parts thereof, and according to all the fashion of it. So was he seven years in building it" (I Kings 6:37,38).

If Solomon's reign began in 971-970 B.C., the fourth year of his reign, when the temple foundation was laid, would be 967-966 B.C. [12,13]

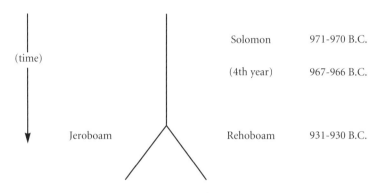

Solomon's Temple and the Egyptian Bondage

After combining the 480-year period between Solomon's temple and the Exodus with the 400-year period of Egyptian bondage, the following picture, which allows for slight differences in dating methods, emerges:

Egyptian Bondage Begins		1847-44 B.C.	Jacob-Israel
	400 YEARS		
Exodus		1447-44 B.C.	Moses
	480 YEARS		
Solomon's Temple		967-64 B.C.	Solomon

Timeline 2000

GATEWAY TO THE PAST
From Solomon to Abraham

The amazing passage from I Kings, along with other Scriptures, opens a gateway to the past that covers over 1000 years—from the building of Solomon's temple back to the time of the Patriarchs; Abraham, Isaac, Jacob and Joseph.

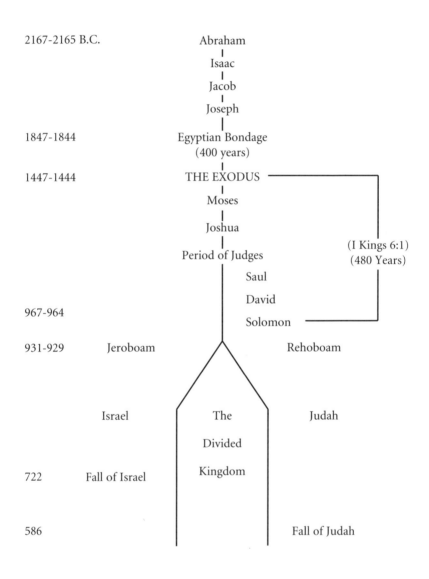

THE TWENTIETH CENTURY
Old Testament Dates Come Alive!

When did Abraham, Isaac and Jacob (Israel) live? Up until this century, dates of Old Testament events remained shrouded in mystery. Amazing new discoveries uncovered during this century in the fields of archaeology and astronomy, and major advances in computer technology have brought the ancient stories of the Bible into focus in a way that previously was not possible.

By using the dates derived by Thiele and by incorporating the chronological information supplied in the Bible, many of the Old Testament events can be dated all the way back to Abraham's birth, around 2166 B.C. Dates prior to Abraham's birth are considered to be less reliable. If 966 B.C. is used as the beginning date of Soloman's Temple, one can work backwards with the help of selected Scriptures to construct a time chart of Old Testament biblical events. [14]

SIGNIFICANT OLD TESTAMENT EVENTS

HISTORIC EVENT	SCRIPTURE	YEARS	DATE	YEARS	SCRIPTURE
Abram born			2166		
(enter Canaan)	Gen. 12:4	75	2091		
Isaac born			2066	100	Gen. 21:5
Jacob born			2006	60	Gen. 25:26
(enter Egypt)			1876	130	Gen. 47:9
Bondage Begins	Gen. 15:13-16 Acts 7:6,7	400	1846		
Bondage Ends (Exodus)			1446	430	Ex. 12:40,41 Gal. 3:17
Solomon's Temple			966	480	I Kings 6:1

The dedication of Solomon's temple and the Exodus from Egypt were defining moments in the history of Israel in which God intervened directly in the affairs of His chosen people. Since the dates of Old Testament events such as the Exodus are not agreed upon by all Bible scholars, a thorough discussion of the date of the Exodus is presented in the following chapter. The date of the Exodus is a pivotal event in the time chart appearing on the back cover.

— 5 —

THE BIBLE AND OLD TESTAMENT EVENTS

"It is well known that archaeology and the Old Testament history cannot be separated without injury to the latter. This is specially true where the latter concerns such a subject as the Exodus and its various historical problems...We are able now to look at the Exodus in a light totally different from that of forty years ago...The evidence adduced has shown...that the Exodus must have taken place about 1445 B.C." [1]

—J. W. Jack (1925)

"According to I Kings 6:1, the Exodus took place 480 years before the fourth year of Solomon's reign, or about 1446...Many who cut themselves loose from the chronological specifics of the Old Testament place the patriarchal period in a general way during the first half of the second millennium B.C. Among such there is no unanimity of opinion in regard to the chronology of the patriarchs." [2]

—Joseph P. Free, Howard F. Vos (1992)

ESCAPE FROM BONDAGE

After confounding the Pharoah of Egypt with a series of ten plagues, God miraculously delivered the children of Israel (formerly Jacob) from Egyptian bondage by parting the waters of the Red Sea. The Exodus of the Jewish people from Egypt nearly 3500 years ago was the cornerstone event which led to the founding of the Jewish nation.

Why is the date of the Exodus important? After reading this chapter, review the back cover of *Timeline 2000*. You will see how God's timing for delivering His chosen people after a 400-year period coincides perfectly with the opening events of Matthew and Luke around 7-4 B.C. following the 400 Silent Years and with the British capture of Palestine and Jerusalem between 1916 and 1919 A.D., at the end of the 400-year Great Reformation.

The Date of the Exodus

When did the Exodus occur? This intriguing and sometimes controversial subject has puzzled archaeologists, Old Testament scholars and Bible students for many centuries. Up until the 20th century, chronologists generally dated the historically significant event between 1200 B.C. and 1650 B.C. [3]

At the turn of the century, around 1910, it was commonly held that the Exodus took place in the 13th century, perhaps about 1230 B.C. [4] Twenty years later, scholars began questioning the late-date view and assigned the Exodus to the 15th century B.C., in the reign of Thotmes III (1490-1435). [5]

This view was reinforced as a result of Professor Garstang's excavations indicating that the city of Jericho was destroyed around 1400 B.C. [6] Taking into account Israel's wandering in the wilderness of Sinai for forty years prior to the conquest of Jericho would place the Exodus from Egypt around the middle of the 15th century. Garstang's findings seemed to be supported by Kathleen Kenyon's excavations (1952-1958) after the final report on her work came out. [7]

Three Views of the Exodus in 1925

According to British Bible scholar J.W. Jack, there were at least three main schools of thought concerning the date of the Exodus when his book, *The Date of the Exodus*, was published in Edinburgh, Great Britain in 1925.

(1) One viewpoint assigned the date of the Exodus to around 1445 B.C. during the 18th Dynasty, just after the long reign of Thutmose III and during that of his son, Amenhotep II. (2) Another view held that the Exodus occurred about 1350 or 1345 B.C. during the reign of Amenhotep IV. (3) The traditional school dated the Exodus during the 19th Dynasty, naming Rameses II (1301-1234 B.C.) as the great oppressor of the Israelites, with the Exodus taking place during the reign of his son, Merenptah (c. 1233-1223 B.C.) or during the reign of one of his immediate successors. [8]

After a lengthy discussion and analysis of all viewpoints, Jack concluded that the Exodus took place about 1445 B.C.:

> "...but this," he says, "does not mean that the Exodus may not have taken place shortly before or after...the view put forward in these pages, which has been advocated by many Biblical scholars and Egyptologists, is the one which best satisfies all the conditions and does least violence to history." [9]

According to Jack, by 1925, astronomers had discovered the date of a total solar eclipse that was visible at Nineveh on June 15 in 763 B.C. This eclipse established all the dates in the Assyrian Canon from 893 to 650 B.C. Assyrian history, which mentions the Battle of Karkar in which Ahab, King of Israel, was present, helped establish the year 970 B.C. for the accession of Solomon and 966 B.C. for the foundation of the temple in his fourth year (I Kings 6:1). [10]

Two Views of the Exodus after 1950

During the last half of the 20th century, two major viewpoints concerning the date of the Exodus have emerged. The historians are divided into two camps. One group supports the early date (c. 1450 B.C.), and the other group holds to the late date (c. 1200-1300 B.C.).

Early-date proponents interpret the Old Testament dating procedures literally, while supporters of the late date prefer to round off the Old Testament numbers and rely more heavily on their interpretation of archaeological findings.

Around 1960, when Dr. Gabriel Hebert wrote *When Israel Came out of Egypt,* he stated that there had been a general return to the thirteenth-century date for the Exodus; however, the dates 1280 or 1270 were preferred rather than 1230 B.C. [11]

Timeline 2000

Scholarly opinion in recent decades that disregards the historical accuracy of the Scriptures supports dates that range from 1225 to 1350 B.C., with 1290 B.C. as the most favored date. [12]

Those who hold to a literal interpretation of the 480 years between the Exodus and the building of Solomon's Temple (I Kings 6:1), however, have held consistently to the early date for the Exodus, 1447-1444 B.C., for nearly 75 years, at least since J. W. Jack's *The Date of the Exodus* was published in 1925.

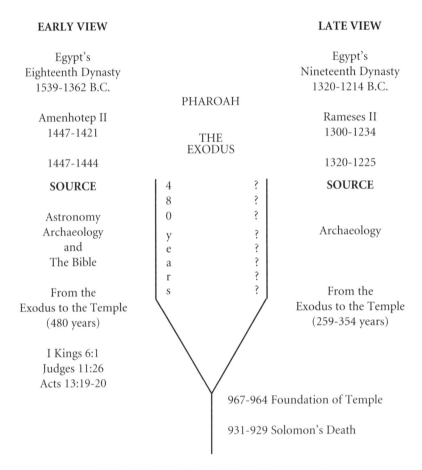

TWO VIEWS OF THE EXODUS [18]

EARLY VIEW		LATE VIEW
Egypt's Eighteenth Dynasty 1539-1362 B.C.		Egypt's Nineteenth Dynasty 1320-1214 B.C.
	PHAROAH	
Amenhotep II 1447-1421	THE EXODUS	Rameses II 1300-1234
1447-1444		1320-1225
SOURCE	480 years / ???????	**SOURCE**
Astronomy Archaeology and The Bible		Archaeology
From the Exodus to the Temple (480 years)		From the Exodus to the Temple (259-354 years)
I Kings 6:1 Judges 11:26 Acts 13:19-20		
	967-964 Foundation of Temple	
	931-929 Solomon's Death	

The Early and Late Views Compared

Although it is beyond the scope of this book to present a detailed discussion of the early and late-date views, a brief summary of each school of thought is presented. For additional study, see the references in the back of the book. [13]

Early Date—This argument insists that the ancient Hebrews knew how to construct a calendar and keep accurate records of time, and that they stated the length of epochs with chronological exactness. It accepts the 480 years of I Kings 6:1 and the statement of Jephthah, a judge who declared that Israel had occupied the land of Canaan for about 300 years (i.e. 1406-1106 B.C.) (Judges 11:26) [14]

Jephthah's defeat of the Ammonites occurred at the end of the twelfth century (i.e., ca. 1100 B.C.), a date which is widely acknowledged. So, then, he is referring to events which came to pass around 1400 B.C. (i.e. when Joshua crossed the Jordan River and began conquering Canaan, c. 1406 B.C.) Allowing 40 years for the Israelites' sojourn in the wilderness brings us to c. 1446 B.C., the early date view for the Exodus.

Late Date—Those who hold this view believe Moses led the Israelites out of bondage during Egypt's nineteenth dynasty, which began around 1318 B.C. under Pharoah Rameses II. [15] This view dismisses I Kings 6:1 as an exaggerated, or even artificial, "twelve generations of forty years each" and prefers a 13th rather than 15th-century B.C. date for the Exodus...Their arguments are primarily archaeological. [16] To accommodate the desire for a later date, the figure 480 is not taken at face value. [17]

The Bible or the Guessing Game?

Should we trust evidence both within and outside the Bible that supports an Exodus date in the middle of the 15th century or rely upon a generalized 13th-century date that rejects biblical evidence and offers no substantive agreement among its proponents?

An excerpt from the *New Unger's Bible Dictionary* reads:

> "... if one carefully surveys all the scriptural evidence, taking into consideration the whole time scheme underlying the Pentateuch and the early history of Israel to the time of Solomon, it is clear that the OT places this great redemptive event around the middle of the fifteenth century B.C. rather than a full century and a half later. Evidence both within and without the Bible in support of this is not easily set aside."[19]

Timeline 2000

Dr. Eugene H. Merrill, Senior Professor of Old Testament Studies at Dallas Theological Seminary, states:

> "…only a drastic resort can explain away the self-evident case for 1446 as the date of the Exodus…Advocates of the late date must disregard all normal and accepted historiographical method and rearrange and reinterpret the only available documentation—the Old Testament itself—if their case is to be made…It should be evident that the arguments usually marshaled in support of a late date for the Exodus and conquest are individuallly and collectively unconvincing and, in fact, run counter to every objective analysis of the biblical date. The Old Testament insists on 1446; denial of that fact is special pleading based on insubstantial evidence." [20]

Dr. J. Barton Payne (1922-1979), former chairman of the Department of Graduate Old Testament at Bob Jones University and professor of Old Testament at Covenant Theological Seminary, supports the 15th-century view of the Exodus in his monumental work *Encyclopedia of Biblical Prophecy*:

> "While legitimate differences of opinion still exist over the precise date for certain events of Biblical history, evidences from astronomy, archaeology, and secular history have made its basic outline increasingly clear. Variations in datings, particularly within the Old Testament, now stem primarily from a reluctance on the part of some critical writers to accept the Scriptural testimony at its face value; and among conservative scholars such pivotal dates as 930 B.C. for the division of the Hebrew kingdom or 1446 for the Exodus are accepted with little difference if any." [21]

The Bible, until proven wrong, is the only legitimate source for determining the date of the Exodus. No historical document or archaeological discovery exists that pinpoints the date of the Exodus except the Bible.

A Bridge Over Troubled Waters

Several sources place the Exodus in March/April of 1446 B.C., based upon a date of 966 for the laying of the foundation of Solomon's

Temple. Other "early" dates generally given are 1445 and 1447 B.C. Allowing for slight differences in dating methods among those who hold to the early view of the Exodus, the date of the Exodus is narrowed to a three-year period: 1447, 1446 or 1445 B.C. [22]

Like a bridge over troubled (historically uncertain) waters, I Kings provides the missing link needed to connect the present with the past: the time period of the Kings (Saul through Zedekiah) with the time of the Patriarchs (Abraham, Isaac, Jacob, Joseph). Adding the 480-year period given in I Kings 6:1 to 967-964 B.C., the fourth year of Solomon's reign, brings us to 1447-1444 B.C., the date of the Exodus.

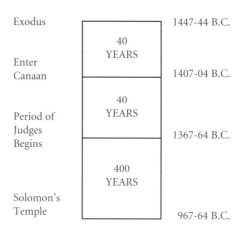

FROM PHYSICAL BONDAGE TO SPIRITUAL FREEDOM

The 480-year period from the Exodus to Solomon's temple began with the children of Israel fleeing physical bondage under the Egyptians and culminated in one of Israel's greatest spiritual moments, the dedication of Solomon's Temple. God spoke with Moses on several occasions at the time of the Exodus (1447-1444 B.C.), and He spoke with Solomon before, during and after completion of the Temple (967-964 B.C.).

The 80-year period following the Exodus is an important part of the timeline on the back cover. Some significant turning points in Israel's history developed during this period which followed the 400 years of Egyptian bondage.

The first half of the 80-year period, Israel's 40 years of wandering in the wilderness, began with the Exodus and ended with Joshua's

Timeline 2000

crossing the Jordan River and entering Canaan. The second half of the 80-year period involved Israel's conquest of Canaan, a lapse into idolatry and God's appointment of Othniel to be the first judge of Israel.

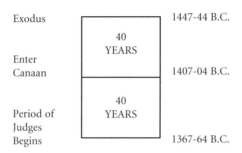

After the Exodus, Israel Wanders in the Wilderness

Due to Israel's refusal to follow the Lord's command and take the land of Canaan, *"...the Lord's anger was kindled against Israel, and he made them wander in the wilderness forty years, until all the generation, that had done evil in the sight of the Lord, was consumed"* (Numbers 32:13). Moses also died during this period of time. When the forty-year period ended, Joshua and all of Israel crossed over the Jordan River and set camp on the east border of Jericho (Joshua 4:14-19). After Israel had conquered most of the land of Canaan, they occupied the land until Joshua and his generation died.

After Joshua Dies, Israel Strays

"And Joshua the son of Nun, the servant of the Lord, died, being an hundred and ten years old...And also all that generation were gathered unto their fathers: and there arose another generation after them, which knew not the Lord, nor yet the works which he had done for Israel. And the children of Israel did evil in the sight of the Lord, and served Baalim" (Judges 2:8-11).

"Therefore the anger of the Lord was hot against Israel, and he sold them into the hand of Chushan-rishathaim King of Mesopotamia: and the children of Israel served Chushan-rishathaim eight years. And when the children of Israel cried unto the Lord, the Lord raised up a deliverer to the children of Israel, who delivered them, even Othniel the son of Kenaz, Caleb's

younger brother. And the spirit of the Lord came upon him, and he judged Israel...and his hand prevailed against Chushan-rishathaim. And the land had rest forty years. And Othniel the son of Kenaz died" (Judges 3:8-11).

The Period of the Judges Begins

Othniel was the first judge of Israel. The exact time of Othniel's judgeship is not certain, however, several sources agree within a seven-year period. One source sets the beginning of his judgeship in 1374 B.C. [23], another in 1373 B.C. [24], and yet another in 1367 B.C. [25] The year 1367 B.C., which is approximately 80 years after the Exodus, is also the year given by Dr. Leon J. Wood (1918-1977), professor of Old Testament Studies and Dean of Grand Rapids Baptist Seminary. [26] Professor Merrill, with Dallas Theological Seminary, believes the period of the judges began after Joshua's death around 1366 B.C. [27]

The period of the judges began a new era in Israel's history and marked the end of the godly leadership provided by Moses and Joshua. The 480-year period which began with Egyptian bondage (1847-1844 B.C.) came to an end as Othniel began his 40-year judgeship (c. 1367-1364 B.C.).

Egyptian Bondage Begins	400 YEARS	1847-44 B.C.
Exodus	40 YEARS	1447-44 B.C.
Enter Canaan	40 YEARS	1407-04 B.C.
Period of Judges Begins		1367-64 B.C.

The above illustration represents the first of three 480-year (400+80) periods in which God has actively intervened in the affairs of the children of Israel. If we include the 400 year period from the Judges

Timeline 2000

to Solomon's Temple, we can see how God has in some cases used 400, 80 and 40 year cycles to carry out His program of redemption with the Jewish people.

Egyptian Bondage Begins		1847-44 B.C.
	400 YEARS	
Exodus		1447-44 B.C.
	40 YEARS	
Enter Canaan		1407-04 B.C.
	40 YEARS	
Period of Judges Begins		1367-64 B.C.
	400 YEARS	
Solomon's Temple		967-64 B.C.

The timeline on the back cover should be reviewed to see how each of the 480-year periods fits into "the big picture" of Israel's history. God's sovereignty in the affairs of His chosen people will become more evident as we journey down through the corridor of time and into the twentieth century.

— 6 —

DOES HISTORY REALLY REPEAT ITSELF?

"Study the past if you would divine the future." [1]
—Confucius

"History is but the unrolled scroll of prophecy." [2]
—James Garfield

"God is in the facts of history as truly as he is in the march of the seasons, the revolutions of the planets, or the architecture of the worlds." [3]
—John Lanahan

Cycles of Time

Historical events sometimes seem to recur in ways that are both fascinating and puzzling. Oliver Wendell Holmes, Jr. remarked: "When I want to understand what is happening today or try to decide what will happen tomorrow, I look back." H.A. Ironside (1876-1951), former pastor at Chicago's Moody Memorial Church and author of *The Four Hundred Silent Years* stated: "History repeats itself in manifold ways, and he who is wise will not despise its instruction."

Certain numbers repeatedly surface in nature and throughout the Bible. Take the number seven, for example. There are seven days in the week, seven colors in the rainbow and seven notes in the musical scale.

When Joshua conquered Jericho, the Lord told him to have seven priests bearing seven trumpets go around the city for seven days and on the seventh day have them circle the city seven times and blow their trumpets. After they followed God's instructions, the walls of Jericho fell down flat (Joshua 6:1-20).

The book of Revelation talks about seven churches, seven spirits, seven golden candlesticks, seven stars, seven lamps, seven seals, seven horns, seven eyes, seven angels, seven trumpets, seven thunders, seven heads, seven mountains, seven kings and seven vials full of the seven last plagues. The number seven has major significance in God's plan for mankind.

Other numbers occur less frequently in the Bible, but in a manner that is either highly suspect as to accuracy or in a manner that is unmistakably part of a master plan orchestrated by the sovereign Creator of the universe. One highly conspicuous instance is the number 400, which surfaces in three significant periods within the past 4,000 years: the Egyptian bondage, the 400 Silent years, and the Great Reformation.

The Egyptian Bondage

Genesis 15:13 reveals that Abram's (whose name was later changed to Abraham) offspring would be strangers in a land that was not theirs and would be servants for 400 years. That period of time has been aptly called "The Egyptian Bondage."

Egyptian Bondage Begins		1847-44 B.C.
	(400)	
Egyptian Bondage Ends		1447-44 B.C.

At the end of this period, the Exodus of God's chosen people took place. Why was the Egyptian bondage 400 years? Why not 390 years or 410 years?

The 400 Silent Years

The next significant 400-year period of time is sandwiched between the close of the Old Testament and the beginning of the New

Testament. This period, roughly from 405 B.C. to 5 B.C., has been called "The 400 Silent Years," "The Period of Silence," "The 400 Year Gap," and "The Intertestimental Period."

The apocryphal writings were penned during "The 400 Silent Years." This four-century gap extends from the time of Nehemiah and Ezra to the gospel accounts of Matthew and Luke, which open prior to the birth of Jesus Christ.

Old Testament Ends		407-404 B.C.
	(400)	
New Testament Begins		7-4 B.C.

The date of the last entries of the Old Testament are not certain. Some believe the last writings were penned around 432 B.C. Others believe the final entry may have been closer to 400 B.C. It appears that some type of activity was present at the temple in Jerusalem in the years leading up to 400 B.C. A writing called the "Elephantine papyri" named Johanan as the high priest of Jerusalem around 407 B.C. [4] According to *The Companion Bible,* the Temple was finished and dedicated in 405 B.C., and Ezra went up to Jerusalem with the Sacred vessels in 404 B.C. [5]

The Great Reformation

The third significant 400-year time period is called "The Great Reformation." Its beginning is generally assigned a date of October 31, 1517, when Martin Luther nailed "The 95 Theses" on the door of All Saints Church at Wittenburg, Germany. The events that led to Luther's action on October 31, 1517, however, had been set in motion months earlier. Four hundred years later brings us to 1917, an amazing year in the annals of history.

Reformation Begins		1516-19 A.D.
	(400)	
Reformation Ends		1916-19 A.D.

Not only was this time span significant on the world scene in terms of religious upheaval, the years surrounding 1517 and 1917 were also significant in the occupation of the land of Palestine by foreign powers.

Ottoman Turks Capture Palestine

On August 24, 1516, Ottoman (Turkish) Sultan Selim I began conquest of northern Palestine on the plain of Marj Dabik located just north of Aleppo (present-day Syria). The Ottoman conquest and sojourn into Palestine lasted two years, from August 1516 to August 1518, when Selim returned to Istanbul, Turkey. During this time, Jerusalem was captured from the Egyptian Mamluks.

The Ottomans went on to conquer the rest of Palestine from the Mamluks of the Egyptian Dynasty and rule Palestine for the next four centuries.

Coincidence or Divine Providence?

Was it coincidental that the Egyptian Bondage, the 400 Silent Years and the Great Reformation were all 400 years in length, or did these three 400-year periods happen at divinely appointed times in history? Refer to these three 400-year periods on the back cover, and you will notice that each 400-year period is followed by an 80-year period. Each 80-year period has been very important in Israel's history.

During the first significant period of 80 years, God delivered the children of Israel from Egypt and gave the Ten Commandments and law to Moses. The second significant period revealed the birth and ministry of Jesus Christ to the Jewish nation. The grace of God offered through Jesus Christ's atoning death on the cross was far superior to the law that was given to Moses. The third significant period of 80 years, which began around the close of World War I, has witnessed the return of the Jewish people to their land after nearly 2000 years of dispersion throughout the world.

These three 80-year periods have been very active times in Israel's history and will be discussed later in the book. However, some of the events need to be addressed in this section. The history of the first 80-year period following the Exodus was discussed in chapter 5. The second period of 80 years, following the "400 Silent Years," opens with the New Testament account of the birth of Jesus Christ.

The Birth of Jesus Christ

The event that heralded the opening of the New Testament was the appearance of the angel Gabriel to Zacharias, the priest, during the days of Herod, the king of Judaea. Gabriel appeared in the temple while Zacharias, the priest, was burning incense and told him that his wife, Elisabeth, would bear a son whose name would be John. Approximately six months later, the heavenly messenger appeared to Mary, and told her she would bring forth a son and would call His name Jesus.

The date of Jesus' birth is not revealed in the Scriptures; however, most scholars assign dates for His birth from 8 B.C. to 1 B.C., with 6 to 4 B.C. being the most prevalent. [6]

The Generation of Christ

The ministry of Jesus began when he was about thirty years old (Luke 3:23), and lasted around three and one half years. Christ said he would suffer many things *"...and be rejected of this generation"* (Luke 17:25). Jesus later pronounced judgment upon the generation that rejected Him and predicted a future destruction of the temple in Jerusalem (Matthew 23:33-24:3).

About forty years after Christ's death, in 70 A.D., the Jewish Temple was destroyed by the Roman army. The prophecy given by Jesus Christ that *"there shall not be left one stone upon another, that shall not be thrown down"* (Mark 13:2) was fulfilled exactly as He had predicted. Historical records reveal that the final judgment of the Jewish people by the Roman army occurred at Masada around 73-75 A.D.

The Life Span of Man

According to Psalm 90:9,10, the average life span of man is seventy to eighty years.

> *"For all our days are passed away in thy wrath: we spend our years as a tale that is told. The days of our years are threescore years and ten; and if by reason of strength they be fourscore years, yet is their strength labour and sorrow; for it is soon cut off, and we fly away."*

The generation of Christ's time would have been between 70 and 80 years old when the destruction of the temple and capture of Masada took place.

Timeline 2000

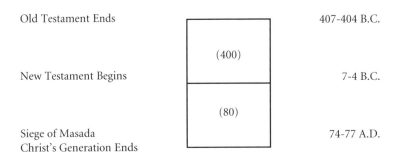

The Diaspora

The destruction of the temple and the final dispersion of the remaining Jews from their land precipitated a period of time called "The Diaspora." The Diaspora refers to "the breaking up and scattering" of the Jews from the land of Palestine.

The Diaspora ended during the nineteenth and twentieth centuries as the Jews began to return to the land of Palestine. Restoration of the nation of Israel in 1948 officially ended displacement from their land; however, many of the Jewish people have continued to return to Israel from countries around the world.

Approximately 400 years after the final siege of Masada (73-75 A.D.), the empire that had controlled Palestine before the birth of Christ, and during the lifetime and generation of Christ, the Roman Empire, came to an end in 476 A.D.

The Fall of Rome

The fall of Rome was long and complicated. The year 476 symbolized the end of the Roman Empire in the West. In this year, the long line of emperors inaugurated by Augustus ended, and the rule of Italy by Germanic leaders began.

In 475 A.D., Romulus Augustulus ("Little Augustus") was elected emperor in the western part of the Roman Empire. The next year, Odovacar, a German commander, deposed Romulus and proclaimed himself head of the government. The overthrow of Romulus Augustulus in 476, whose name ironically came from the founder of Rome and the founder of the Empire, marked the traditional date for the "fall" of the Roman Empire.[7]

The fall of the Roman Empire 400 years after the Romans dispersed the Jews from their land is not included in the timeline on the back cover due to space constraints. However, this period of time coincides with the 400-year period prior to Solomon's Temple that was discussed in the previous chapter. In both cases, an important 80-year period of Jewish history was sandwiched in between two 400-year periods of time. Are these cycles of time accidental, or are they evidence of God's intervention in the historical affairs of mankind?

Old Testament Ends		407-404 B.C.
	(400)	
New Testament Begins		7-4 B.C.
	(80)	
Siege of Masada Christ's Generation Ends The Diaspora Begins		74-77 A.D.
	(400)	
Roman Empire Ends		474-477 A.D.

Following the second 80-year period that ended with the Siege of Masada and the dispersion of the Jews (the Diaspora), the third period of 80 years, which followed "The Great Reformation," began as World War I came to a close.

Great Britain Captures Palestine

Precisely 400 years after Selim's capture of Palestine, history seemed to repeat itself; however, this time the British forces began the offensive against Palestine on August 4, 1916, with the capture of Romani from the Ottoman Turks at the northern border of the Sinai Desert.

Turks Capture Palestine		1516-1519 A.D.
	400 Years	
British Capture Palestine		1916-1919 A.D.

This campaign, like the Ottoman conquest 400 years earlier, also lasted two years, with the British capture of Palestine completed in September and October of 1918, just prior to the end of World War I on November 11, 1918.

General Allenby Takes Over

The initial push by Great Britain in 1916 to take Palestine from the Ottoman Turks met with considerable resistance and was not successful. When the British began their second offensive under General Allenby, Beersheba was the first major city to be taken on October 31, 1917. Allenby's first victory at Beersheba was exactly 400 years after Martin Luther nailed the "95 Theses" to the door of the church at Wittenburg, Germany.

The Dan and Beersheba Connection

During the time of the judges, kings and prophets, Dan and Beersheba were considered the northern and southern borders of the twelve tribes of Israel. These two cities were mentioned together on numerous occasions when Israel and Judah were described collectively as a nation.

> *"Then all the children of Israel went out, and the congregation was gathered together as one man, from Dan even to Beersheba, with the land of Gilead, unto the Lord in Mizpeh"* (Judges 20:1).
>
> *"For the king said to Joab the captain of the host, which was with him, Go now through all the tribes of Israel, from Dan even to Beersheba, and number ye the people, that I may know the number of the people"* (II Samuel 24:2).
>
> *"So they established a decree to make proclamation throughout all Israel, from Beersheba even to Dan, that they should come to keep the passover unto the Lord God of Israel at Jerusalem: for they had not done it of a long time in such sort as it was written"* (II Chronicles 30:5).

Beersheba: Gateway to the Holy Land

Beersheba was the home of Abraham, Isaac and Jacob for many years up until the time Jacob (Israel) and his sons went to Egypt to escape the famine. Being the southernmost city in Palestine, Beersheba was considered "the gateway to the Holy Land."

One writer described the highly significant capture of Beersheba by General Allenby in the following manner:

> "Dawn was approaching with no sound from the ancient city (Beersheba) where Abraham made the covenant with Abimelech—the southern gateway to the Holy Land before which the silent hosts were closing in…" [8]

Ironically, the British War Cabinet's acceptance of the Balfour Declaration on the last day of October, 1917, also coincided with General Allenby's move to retake Palestine after 400 years of control by the Ottoman Empire. Was the precise timing of these events, 400 years apart, coincidental, or was God's sovereign hand involved?

The Balfour Declaration

The Balfour Declaration, issued on November 2, 1917, two days after the British War Cabinet approved the document, was the first official public statement by Great Britain that openly stated the need for a home for the Jewish people.

> "DEAR LORD ROTHSCHILD,—I have much pleasure in conveying to you, on behalf of His Majesty's Government, the following declaration of sympathy with Jewish Zionist aspirations which has been submitted to, and approved by, the Cabinet.
>
> "His Majesty's Government view with favour the establishment in Palestine of a national home for the Jewish people, and will use their best endeavours to facilitate the achievement of this object, it being clearly understood that nothing shall be done which may prejudice the civil and religious rights of existing non-Jewish communities in Palestine or the rights and political status enjoyed by Jews in any other country.
>
> "I should be grateful if you would bring this declaration to the knowledge of the Zionist Federation.
>
> "Yours sincerely,
>
> "Arthur James Balfour." [9]

The Balfour Declaration was considered highly instrumental in helping bring about the reestablishment of Israel as a nation and was mentioned in the Proclamation of Independence read on May 14, 1948, the day before Israel's statehood took effect. The importance of the Balfour Declaration was echoed in writing shortly after its inception:

> "The Declaration by the British Government in favour of the establishment in Palestine of a National Home for the Jewish people constitutes the greatest event in the history of the Jews since their dispersion." [10]

Another statement by a high-level military officer in Palestine during the years of the British Mandate stresses the importance attached to the Balfour Declaration:

> "Seldom has a single sentence constituting an international engagement provoked so much controversy and so much partisan writing as this brief letter, the Balfour Declaration, addressed by the Foreign Secretary of the British Government to a representative English Jew, Lord Rothschild. It was for thirty years the foundation of British policy towards a Jewish National Home in Palestine, the basis of the mandate conferred on England by the League of Nations for the government of Palestine, and the precursor of the establishment of the State of Israel." [11]

Allenby Captures Jerusalem

"On the 9th of December, 1917, the whole world was thrilled by the news of the capture of Jerusalem and, with the obvious exception of the enemy, rejoiced in the knowledge that this City of Contention, sacred alike to Christian, Mohammedan and Jew, had been freed for ever, after four centuries of oppression and misrule, from the yoke of the Turk." [12]

Two days later, on December 11, 1917, General Allenby and the British forces entered Jerusalem without firing a shot. The triumphant entry into Jerusalem was exactly 401 years after Jerusalem and Gaza was secured by the Ottoman Turks on December 11, 1516.

Does History Really Repeat Itself?

A New Era Begins

Allenby's conquest signaled the beginning of a new era in Palestine and the Middle East. The year 1917 also held major significance for the Jewish people throughout Europe and Asia. One source summarized the changes that were taking place:

"For...the majority of European Jewry, the Middle Ages did not actually end until 1917. However, echoes of a new age had long since permeated their 'pale of settlement,' stimulating the bearers of the oldest living culture of Europe to seek new horizons." [13]

Times of Change

The events that surrounded the years 1517 and 1917 are summarized in the chart below. The periods of 1516-1519 and 1916-1919 were times of significant change for Europe, Asia and the Mideast.

Turks Enter Palestine		August 24, 1516
Selim I Captures Jerusalem		Dec. 11, 1516
REFORMATION BEGINS	(1516-1519)	
Luther's 95 Theses		October 31, 1517
Turks Secure Palestine		August, 1518
	400 Years	
British Enter Palestine		August 4, 1916
Allenby Captures Beersheba		October 31, 1917
Balfour Decl. Approved		October 31, 1917
REFORMATION ENDS	(1916-1919)	
Jerusalem Captured		Dec. 8-11, 1917
British Secure Palestine		Sept. 19-31, 1918
World War I Ends		Nov. 11, 1918

The Zionist Movement Takes Hold

During the latter years of the 19th century, Theodore Hertzl, father of the Zionist movement, actively worked to establish a new home for the Jewish people, who had been scattered throughout the world for nearly 2,000 years. The First Zionist Congress, designed to establish a home for the Jews in Palestine, was held in August 1897 in Basel, Switzerland.

Israel Becomes a Nation

Unprecedented events at the turn of the century began to set the stage for an untimely actor, the Jewish people, to return to the Middle East stage. The events that developed during World War I, especially the conquest of Palestine by the British, opened a door in the Middle East that would allow the Jews to eventually return in large numbers to the land of Palestine.

In western Europe, "Chaim Weizmann was elected President of the British Zionist Federation in February 1917, enabling him to propose officially that the British government should make a public commitment to support a Jewish homeland in Palestine." [14]

On May 15, 1948, the nation of Israel was reborn. This event had been alluded to by the Prophet Isaiah more than 2500 years ago.

"Shall the earth be made to bring forth in one day? or shall a nation be born at once? for as soon as Zion travailed, she brought forth her children. Shall I bring to the birth, and not cause to bring forth? saith the Lord: shall I cause to bring forth, and shut the womb? saith thy God" (Isaiah 66:8,9).

Does History Repeat Itself?

Again, refer to the three 80-year periods of Jewish history on the back cover. Is history repeating itself in a random fashion, or is God actively involved in the affairs of the nation of Israel? God said in Genesis 12:2,3:

"...I will make of thee a great nation, and I will bless thee, and make thy name great; and thou shalt be a blessing: And I will bless them that bless thee, and curse him that curseth thee: and in thee shall all families of the earth be blessed."

The nations of the world have been pressuring Israel into giving up land that rightfully belongs to them. Jerusalem is also quickly becoming a divisive issue in world politics. The Lord said in Zechariah 12:3-9:

> *"...in that day will I make Jerusalem a burdensome stone for all people: all that burden themselves with it shall be cut in pieces, though all the people of the earth be gathered against it...And it shall come to pass in that day, that I will seek to destroy all the nations that come against Jerusalem."*

The prophecy given in Zechariah seems to be developing before our very eyes. The 80-year period we are currently living in may be a prelude to the end-time prophecies given in the books of Daniel and Revelation. Does history repeat itself? The next chapter reveals an amazing time cycle that is additional proof that God has been actively involved in Israel's history!

7

THE THREE RETURNS OF ISRAEL

"Now the sojourning of the children of Israel, who dwelt in Egypt, was four hundred and thirty years. And it came to pass at the end of the four hundred and thirty years, even the self same day it came to pass, that all the hosts of the Lord went out from the land of Egypt."

—Exodus 12: 40,41

"Thus saith the Lord of hosts, the God of Israel, unto all that are carried away captives, whom I have caused to be carried away from Jerusalem unto Babylon…that after seventy years be accomplished at Babylon, I will visit you, and perform my good word toward you, in causing you to return to this place."

—Jeremiah 29: 4,10

"Behold I will gather them out of all countries, whither I have driven them in mine anger, and in my fury, and in great wrath; and I will bring them again unto this place, and I will cause them to dwell safely; And they shall be my people, and I will be their God."

—Jeremiah 32:37,38

THE RETURN FROM EGYPT

Israel has been absent from the land of Palestine on three different occasions during the past 4000 years. God told Abraham his seed (offspring) would be a stranger in a land that was not theirs, and they would be afflicted for four hundred years (Genesis 15:13-21). The first departure of Israel (Jacob) from Canaan (later called Palestine), was to escape a famine that had come upon the land. When Israel (Jacob) and his seventy descendents entered Egypt around 1876 B.C., Joseph was second in command of Egypt.

The offspring of Jacob (Israel), under Joseph's oversight, prospered in the land of Egypt. Eventually, a Pharoah came to power that *"knew not Joseph"* (Exodus 1:8) and began acting harshly towards the Israelites. For the next 400 years (c. 1846-1446 B.C.), the children of Israel served Egypt in *"a land that is not theirs"* as God had told Abraham. The Exodus of Israel from Egypt around 1446 B.C. was the first return of the children of Israel back to the land of Canaan (Palestine).

According to the writer of Exodus, the departure of the children of Israel occurred 430 years after Israel (Jacob) entered Egypt.

> *"Now the sojourning of the children of Israel, who dwelt in Egypt, was four hundred and thirty years. And it came to pass at the end of the four hundred and thirty years, even the self same day it came to pass, that all the hosts of the Lord went out from the land of Egypt"* (Exodus 12: 40,41).

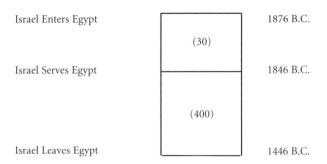

God's plan for the Jewish people covered exactly 430 years to the day and culminated in an event that has historically been called "The Exodus."

THE RETURN FROM BABYLON

Israel's second return took place at the end of seventy years of captivity which began around 606 B.C. after King Nebuchadnezzar of Babylon entered the land of Palestine and took many of the Jews, including Daniel, back to Babylon.

Solomon's Temple		966 B.C.
	(360)	
Jews Taken to Babylon		606 B.C.
	(70)	
Jews Return from Babylon		536 B.C.

As God had prophesied through the prophet Jeremiah, a group of Jewish people returned seventy years later, in 536 B.C. (Daniel 9:2). Israel's return from Babylon in 536 B.C. was 430 years after the foundation of Solomon's Temple was laid in 966 B.C.

THE RETURN FROM THE WORLD

On February 16, 1518 A.D., Selim I, Turkish Sultan and head of the Ottoman Empire from 1512 to 1520, solidified control over Palestine by appointing Janbardi al-Ghazali "governor over all southern Syria and Palestine, from Damascus to Jerusalem, Amman, and Gaza."[1] This official appointment was the final act of Selim I to secure and maintain control of Palestine.[2,3]

After making additional appointments to secure the cities of Tripoli, Amman and Aleppo, Selim left Palestine in August of 1518 for Istanbul, Turkey, never to return again.[4] The land of Palestine was to remain under Ottoman control for the next 400 years.

From 1518 to 1918, the Ottoman Empire, which stretched from Southeastern Europe to Palestine and across Northern Africa, continued to be the dominant force in the Mideast. After 400 years of control of Jerusalem and the land of Palestine by the Turks, World War I brought the Allied forces into the Mediterranean arena.

Timeline 2000

In September of 1918, General Allenby of Great Britain, commander of the British forces in the Mideast, began the last major offensive in Palestine after having taken Jerusalem from the Ottoman army in December of the previous year. On October 26, Aleppo was taken, and four days later, the Ottoman Empire surrendered with the signing of the Armistice of Mudros. [5]

On November 11, 1918, the fighting stopped, and World War I came to an end. Control of Palestine by the British was now secure, and the land of Palestine was to remain under the supervision of Great Britain for the next thirty years. Rabbi Eliezer Ben-Yehuda of Jerusalem stated: "I was born in what was called Palestine-Eretz Israel (i.e. "Palestine, the Land of Israel!" That was its legal designation, as found on the official stationery, the coins and stamps issued there from 1921 to 1948)—during the time of the British Mandate." [6]

Ottoman Occupation	(400)	1518 A.D.
British Occupation		1918 A.D.
Rebirth of Israel	(30)	1948 A.D.

In 1948, the British Mandate to oversee the land of Palestine expired, and the nation of Israel miraculously came back to life after nearly 2000 years of dispersion (the Diaspora) throughout the nations of the world. Four hundred years of control by the Ottoman Turks and thirty years of occupation by the British ended with Israel's official rebirth and return to national status on May 15, 1948.

THE THREE RETURNS OF ISRAEL COMPARED

Dr. John F. Walvoord, in his book, *Major Bible Prophecies*, summarizes Israel's three departures and three returns from many nations throughout the world:

> "Just as both Israel's first dispersion into Egypt and second dispersion into Assyria and Babylon were fulfilled with Israel's

literal return to the Promised Land, so the Old Testament predicted a third and world-wide dispersion, the extent of which was never realized in Israel's earlier dispersions…Israel's ultimate dispersion was anticipated by Christ when he prophesied the destruction of the temple: '*I tell you the truth, not one stone here will be left on another; every one will be thrown down*' " (Matt. 24:2). [7]

Israel's third and final return to their land is described in Isaiah 43:5,6:

"Fear not: for I am with thee: I will bring thy seed from the east, and gather thee from the west; I will say to the north, Give up; and to the south, Keep not back: bring my sons from far, and my daughters from the ends of the earth…"

Isaiah's prophecy implies a worldwide regathering, which could only have taken place after a worldwide dispersion. A worldwide dispersion occurred only one time in Jewish history; after the conquest of Jerusalem by the Roman army in 70 A.D.

The three returns of Israel from Egypt, Babylon and the world occurred after a 430 year period in all three cases. The possibility of Israel planning their own return to the land of Palestine at the end of three 430 year periods of time, when they were not in control of their own destiny, is at the least "mind boggling" and at the most, God's sovereign design and plan for his chosen people; the children of Israel.

8

ISRAEL

God's Prophetic Clock

"…*God's timepiece is not B-U-L-O-V-A or T-I-M-E-X, but God's timepiece is I-S-R-A-E-L.*" [1]

—J. Vernon McGee

"*Israel is God's time clock. If you want to know what is going on in the world today, observe carefully what is happening in Israel. Not one word of God will fail in regard to Israel…God watches over His Word to perform it. And because His promises for Israel will not fail, neither will His promises to you.*" [2]

—Kay Arthur

"*Israel is in the vortex of last day events…I believe that Israel is God's time clock. The midnight hour approaches! O What an exciting prospect! What a wonderful hope!*" [3]

—Charles Halff

Israel, long considered by Bible scholars to be God's prophetic clock, operated silently from the first century A.D. following the destruction of the Jewish Temple in Jerusalem until the first half of the nineteenth century. Then a movement known as Zionism began to take hold and awaken the desire for a homeland in the hearts of many of the Jewish people in the decades leading up to the twentieth century.

The clock began to tick louder and louder as world events and God's unmistakable intervention created a home for the Jews during the closing years of World War I. Official national status came on the heels of World War II as the nation of Israel was proclaimed on May 15, 1948.

One observer remarked that World War I prepared the land (Palestine) for the people (Jews), and World War II prepared the people for the land. Dr. Theodor Herzl (1860-1904), a Jewish leader and founder of the Zionist movement, said: "There is a land without a people. There is a people without a land. Give the land without a people to the people without a land." [4]

> "British scholar Ian MacPherson points out that it was an evangelical Christian Jew, William Heckler, who wooed and won to Zionism, professor Theodor Herzl, a Jew from Budapest, in the late nineteenth century. Herzl in turn won to Zionism scientist Chaim Weizmann, the first president of Israel, and Weizmann recruited David Ben-Gurion, the first prime minister of Israel." [5]

Israel's attainment of national status after 1900 years of worldwide dispersion is unprecedented in the history of the world. A Gentile professor of archaeology at Johns Hopkins University, Dr. William F. Albright, commented:

> "It is without parallel in the annals of human history that a nation carried into captivity for seventy years should return to resume its national life, that after nearly six hundred years this same nation should again be scattered worldwide for nearly two thousand years and retain its identity, and that this people should then return to rebuild its ancient homeland and achieve statehood among the family of nations...Many non-prophetic souls, of whom I was one, declared that such a thing was impossible...And yet we have seen it. Since the words of the Old Testament prophets have been literally fulfilled we should expect the remainder of their predictions concerning the nation Israel likewise to be fulfilled." [6]

Israel's return to the land of Palestine during this century, coupled with miraculous military victories during the Mideast wars of 1948, 1956, 1967 and 1973, and Israel's rapid rise to world status in commerce, technology and military strength, serve as strong evidence that God is once again openly intervening in the affairs of His chosen people.

WHERE ARE WE ON GOD'S TIMETABLE?
Is it Possible to Know?

The time of the first coming of Jesus Christ, the Messiah, was revealed to Daniel the prophet (9:24-26) over 500 years before the event was to take place. The prophetic vision given to Daniel by the angel Gabriel, sometimes called Daniel's seventy weeks, was a 490 year cycle and time table (70 weeks and 7 years per week equals 490 years) that would reveal the Messiah to the Jewish people.

The only authoritative religious figure living around 30 A.D. that could fulfill the prophecy given to Daniel was Jesus Christ. Will the second coming of Christ involve a 490 year cycle? The Scriptures do not give any clues concerning the precise time of the second coming of Christ back to earth, so any projections using a 490 year timecycle would be highly speculative.

If God keeps time by the Jews, and the Jewish people have been brought back to their land during this century, where does that place us on God's timetable? What does the future hold? The answers to these intriguing questions are not yet fully evident; however, the end-time scenario as described in the Bible appears to be falling in place before our very eyes. Prophetic events predicted in the Bible many times cast their shadow backward in time prior to their fulfillment. We should be watching for these prophetic shadows, many of which are already present in the world today.

If Israel is God's prophetic timepiece, perhaps Jerusalem is the hour hand, and the Temple Mount is the minute hand. According to Scripture, Jerusalem is "the apple of God's eye" (Lam. 2:18), and the restoration of the Temple (Rev. 11:1,2) will play an important role in the timing of end-time events (Matt. 24:15-22).

THE PAST, THE PRESENT AND THE FUTURE:
A New 80-Year Time Cycle?

If the periods following the 400 years of Egyptian bondage and the 400 Silent Years between the Old and New Testaments repeat, a new

Timeline 2000

80-year cycle should have started between 1916 and 1919. All three 80-year periods have been significant in the history of Israel. These periods were discussed in earlier chapters; however, some additional commentary will help show how events during these periods helped shape the history of Israel and the whole world.

THE FIRST 80-YEAR PERIOD:
Exodus to the Judges

Following the 400-year period of Egyptian bondage, Moses and the children of Israel crossed the Red Sea and entered the Sinai Peninsula. Moses received the Ten Commandments from God on Mount Sinai and brought them down from the mountain for Israel to follow.

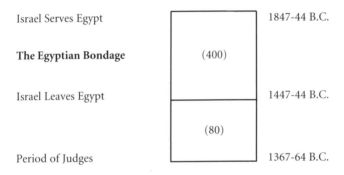

Israel Serves Egypt		1847-44 B.C.
The Egyptian Bondage	(400)	
Israel Leaves Egypt		1447-44 B.C.
	(80)	
Period of Judges		1367-64 B.C.

When Israel refused to go into Canaan and take the land as God had commanded, God made them wander in the wilderness for forty years until the rebellious generation had died. Joshua took command at the end of the forty years and led Israel across the Jordan River into the Promised Land. After the generation of Joshua died, the next generation fell into idolatry, and God appointed the first judge of Israel, Othniel, to judge His people.

THE SECOND 80-YEAR PERIOD:
Birth of Christ to the Diaspora

At the end of "The 400 Silent Years," the New Testament opened with the birth of John the Baptist and Jesus Christ. At around thirty years of age, Jesus began a three and one-half year ministry of teaching and performing miracles that changed the course of human history.

At the end of His ministry, Christ gave His life up (Mark 10:45) and allowed the Roman army to crucify Him on a cross (Acts 2:23).

Three days later, He arose from the dead and appeared to many witnesses before His ascension back to Heaven. Christ is now at the right hand of God where He makes intercession for us (Romans 8:34).

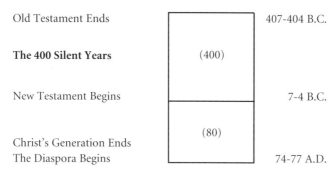

Old Testament Ends		407-404 B.C.
The 400 Silent Years	(400)	
New Testament Begins		7-4 B.C.
	(80)	
Christ's Generation Ends		
The Diaspora Begins		74-77 A.D.

Following Christ's death, burial and resurrection, the twelve apostles began their ministry. The books of the New Testament were written during the remainder of the century, and the Gospel message of salvation through faith in Jesus Christ was spread throughout much of the known world. As prophesied by Jesus in Matthew 24, Mark 13 and Luke 21, in the Olivet Discourse, the Temple was destroyed in 70 A.D. with *"not one stone left upon another."*

The eighth decade of the first century A.D. also witnessed the siege of Masada, the last stronghold of the Jews, around 73-75 A.D. As prophesied in Matthew 23:34-24:2, destruction had come to the Temple and the generation that had rejected Christ. The remaining Jews were dispersed throughout the world (the Diaspora) and were mostly absent from the land of Palestine up until the middle of the 19th century. These things came upon the Jewish people because they would not accept the Messiah and did not recognize the time of their visit from God (Daniel 9:24-26, Luke 19:41-44).

THE THIRD 80-YEAR PERIOD:
World War I to the Next Millennium

As the 400-year period of the Great Reformation came to a close with the end of World War I, a new era had begun.

> "The Middle East, as we know it from today's headlines, emerged from decisions made by the Allies during and after the First World War." [7]
>
> David Fromkin

Timeline 2000

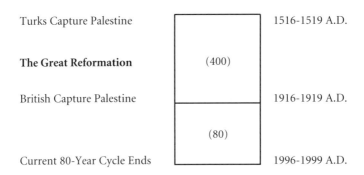

Turks Capture Palestine		1516-1519 A.D.
The Great Reformation	(400)	
British Capture Palestine		1916-1919 A.D.
	(80)	
Current 80-Year Cycle Ends		1996-1999 A.D.

New discoveries and technologies emerged in the first World War that revolutionized the industrialized nations of the world. More sophisticated methods of warfare were developed, and innovative products began to appear in the marketplace.

> "The year 1918 marks the beginning of the world of today. Through such trivial and mundane accessories of current living as the factory—made cigarette, the wristwatch, the flashlight, the safety razor—all of them hardly more than curiosities before World War I... Earlier wars had celebrated the foot soldier as the hero of battles, but from World War I emerged the pursuit pilot, above all others—the shining knight of combat—the airplane itself as the most glorious of all possible weapons...there is little doubt that the use of the truck as a vehicle of mass transportation had its beginnings in the war...A look back at the year 1918, with the advantage of fifty years of hindsight, reveals it as a year when the shape of today's world can be quite clearly discerned." [8]
>
> Joseph Carter

In the Mideast, the issuance of the Balfour Declaration in 1917 and the capture of Palestine by the British army restored new life to the Jewish people who longed for a return to their homeland. Great Britain was given a mandate by the Allied Powers in April 1920 to oversee the development of Palestine.

Mideast Wars and Commotions

World War I and World War II brought forth a new era in modern warfare that, for the first time in history, made it possible for Christ's prophecy in Mark 13:8 to be fulfilled:

> *"For nation shall rise against nation, and kingdom against kingdom: and there shall be earthquakes in divers places, and there shall be famines and troubles: these are the beginnings of sorrows."*

The nations and kingdoms of the world, no longer isolated from each other's problems, were forming new alliances and beginning global commercial adventures.

Following the Holocaust and the atrocities of World War II, the British relinquished control of Palestine, and the nation of Israel was reborn on May 15, 1948. Arab countries strongly resisted Israel's desire for statehood and attacked the new nation immediately. Although the odds of surviving were slim, a miraculous victory was achieved by Israel. Additional wars followed in 1956, 1967 and 1973 in which Israel was again victorious. During the June war of 1967, Israel captured the Arab sector of Jerusalem, including the old walled city.

Peace and Security Pacts

During 1977, the first direct peace negotiations between Israel and an Arab state took place. On March 26, 1979, the Israel-Egypt Peace Treaty was signed in Washington, D.C. by President Anwar Sadat of Egypt and Prime Minister Menachem Begin of Israel with President Jimmy Carter presiding. Additional peace agreements between Israel and Arab states have been negotiated and signed during the last two decades of this century.

The words "peace and security" and "peace and prosperity" have been used frequently in recent years in anticipation of a permanent peace in the Mideast. The expressions "peace and safety" or "peace and security" are also used in the Bible to describe the period of time prior to the Lord's return to the earth.

> *"For the Lord himself shall descend from heaven with a shout, with the voice of the archangel, and with the trump of God: and the dead in Christ shall rise first: Then we which are alive and remain shall be caught up together with them in the clouds, to meet the Lord in the air: and so shall we ever be with the Lord. Wherefore comfort one another with these words.*

> *But of the times and seasons, brethren, ye have no need that I write unto you. For yourselves know perfectly that the day of the Lord so cometh as a thief in the night. For when they shall say, peace and safety; then sudden destruction cometh upon them, as travail upon a woman with child; and they shall not escape...Therefore let us not sleep, as do others; but let us watch and be sober."*
>
> I Thessalonians 4:16-5:6

Threshold to the Next Millennium
1996-1999

A wood or metal threshold is usually placed underneath the outside doors in a building to keep cold or hot air from coming inside. The threshold represents the dividing point between the inside and the outside. Between 1996 and 1999, we will pass across a threshold of time that opens to the next century and the next millennium.

As we exit the current 480-year (400+80) period and enter a new cycle, what will the future hold? Will the 480-year cycle continue? What will happen after we pass across the threshold and enter the 21st century remains to be seen; however, certain trends have clearly been established.

Many of the nations of the world are being linked together financially as they move towards "A New World Order." Financial transactions will be monitored by large computer systems that keep dossiers (detailed information) on customers under the guise of maintaining essential credit records. Credit cards are commonplace in today's society, and monitoring and tracking devices are currently being used to follow prisoners and locate lost animals and stolen property.

As soon as it becomes socially acceptable, monitoring devices will be implanted in people. Buying and selling of goods and services will be much more convenient, theft of money and stolen property will be reduced or eliminated, and location of missing persons with satellite tracking systems will be justifiable benefits to a modern society. Commercial transactions will be more convenient, cost efficient, and time saving to the consumer.

This coming world-wide economic system, which will eventually be controlled by a diabolical world leader, resembles the system of buying and selling described in the book of Revelation that will be prevalent shortly before Christ returns to set up His Kingdom:

> *"And he causeth all, both small and great, rich and poor, free and bond, to receive a mark in their right hand, or in their foreheads: And that no man might buy or sell, save he that had the mark, or the name of the beast, or the number of his name. Here is wisdom. Let him that hath understanding count the number of the beast: for it is the number of a man; and his number is six hundred threescore and six"* (Revelation 13:16-18).

A system of control over who buys and sells food, clothing, housing and other merchandise will be in place for the first time since the prophecy was given to John nearly two thousand years ago on the island of Patmos. This is yet another indication that God's prophetic plan for mankind, as described in the book of Revelation, looms ominously on the horizon!

An Overview of the Timeline 2000 Chart

The chart at the end of this chapter and on the back cover represents the last 4000 years of Jewish history. Most of the events in Israel's history, listed on the chart, have been discussed; however, a few unique features need to be pointed out.

The three 480-year (400+80) "Significant Periods" on the left side of the timeline represent major turning points in Israel's history. Directly across from the "Significant Periods," under the heading "Jewish History," are the corresponding events in Israel's history.

Between the three 480-year (400+80) "Significant Periods" are periods that are important but appear to be less significant than the 400+80-year cycles. For example, the Period of Judges, Kings, Prophets, Exile and Return is represented by a 960-year (480+480) span of time, and the period labeled the Diaspora is represented by a 1440-year (480+480+480) span of time.

The 480-year divisions given in both examples do not seem to have any significance other than providing an amazingly smooth and supernatural transition between the eight consecutive 480-year cycles listed under the "Date" heading. Perhaps God's "prophetic clock" is ticking silently during these supernatural interludes.

The Big Picture

From the Old Testament patriarchs Abraham, Isaac, Jacob and Joseph, who lived around the year 2000 B.C., to the birth of Christ and His ministry 2000 years later, to the 20th century in which we are now living, 4000 years later, God has miraculously and sometimes mysteriously brought His chosen people, the Jews, through many trials and tribulations and has been actively involved in preserving the racial identity of the Jewish people.

Many prophecies in the Bible concerning the end times could not be fulfilled until the Jews had returned to their land. Therefore, the restoration of Israel to the land of Palestine is perhaps the single greatest sign heralding the soon return of Jesus Christ to set up His kingdom. The next millennium will be the fifth since the birth of Jacob (Israel), the fourth since King David established Jerusalem as his capitol and the third since the birth of Jesus Christ.

To the serious and perceptive student of God's Word, God's prophetic clock, Israel, is no longer silent, but is now ticking loud and clear. God's Word warns us repeatedly not to be asleep spiritually, but to watch and be prepared for His return. When the alarm on God's prophetic clock sounds (God's trumpet), will you be ready?

Israel: God's Prophetic Clock!

SIGNIFICANT PERIODS	DATE			JEWISH HISTORY
OLD TESTMENT PATRIARCHS Abraham, Isaac, Jacob, Joseph	2000 B.C.			BIRTH OF JACOB-ISRAEL Israel Moves to Egypt
The Egyptian Bondage	400	1847-44	480	Israel Serves Egypt (400 Years) Israel Leaves Egypt
THE EXODUS	80	1447-44		LAW: TEN COMMANDMENTS
		1367-64	480	Period of Judges, Kings, Prophets, Exile, Return
		886	480	
The 400 Silent Years	400	407-4	480	Old Testament Ends (400 Years) New Testament Begins
THE BIRTH OF CHRIST	80	7-4		GRACE: JESUS CHRIST
		74-77	480	(The Diaspora)
		557	480	
		1037	480	
		1516-19		
The Great Reformation	400	1916-19		Turks Capture Palestine (400 Years) British Capture Palestine
World War I 1914-1918 British Enter Palestine 1916 British Take Palestine 1918 World War II 1939-1945 British Leave Palestine 1948 Mideast Wars & Commotions Peace & Security Pacts 1948 to Present	80		480	Balfour Declaration 1917 Jerusalem Captured 1917 **ISRAEL BECOMES A NATION** 1948 **ENTERING** Third Millennium Since Birth of Christ; Fourth Millennium Since King David's Reign Began; Fifth Millennium Since Birth of Israel
NEW MILLENNIUM BEGINS	2000 A.D.	1996-99		NEW "1000 YEARS" BEGINS

— 9 —

THE TIME OF THE END

Have We Arrived?

"…There is only one authoritative book in the world that accurately predicts what is going to happen in the future—and that is the Bible." [1]

—Billy Graham

"If anything would convince me that there must be a God, it would be the present-day fulfillment of Bible prophecy." [2]

—Marlin Maddoux

"Prophetic events are accelerating. I used to get excited if I saw a significant event in prophecy occur every three or four years. Now you can hardly pick up a newspaper or look at a television newscast without seeing something that directly relates to the predicted scenario of events that would come together in concert just before the return of Christ." [3]

—Hal Lindsey

The slogan "the end is near" has been used by various individuals and groups in the past when they felt the human race was facing imminent extinction. These people have cried wolf for so long that most of the world has become indifferent to warnings of coming judgment, and many have disregarded the one tried and proven source for prophetic information—the Bible.

The return of Israel to Palestine, the movement towards a "new world order," the worldwide breakdown of moral and social values and the appearance of many converging Bible prophecies during this century should prompt us to ask questions such as: *Are we living in the time of the end?*, and *Is it possible to know when the end is near?*

As mentioned earlier, this world is undergoing a rapid metamorphosis into a world-based economy and society that will be much different in the 21st century. The movement towards a new world order and the amazing, lightning-like changes that are reshaping technology will play a major role in forging the economic and political structure of the world.

These changes, many of which are helping bring about pre-Noah, pre-Babel and pre-Sodom conditions in the world, will almost certainly result in God's intervention into the affairs of this planet.

What in the World is Going On?

The Book of books, the Bible, has much to say about end-time events, and the book of Daniel supplies the key verse necessary for understanding the period known as *"the time of the end:"*

> *"But thou, O Daniel, shut up the words, and seal the book, even to the time of the end: many shall run to and fro, and knowledge shall be increased"* (Daniel 12:4).

Do the conditions of "many running to and fro" and "increased knowledge" apply to today's society?

Accelerated Travel. Up until the 19th century, man's major source of transportation was by foot, boat or horse, with a top speed of around forty miles per hour. In 1807, that began to change when the first economical steamboat, the Clermont, made its maiden voyage up the Hudson River. The 1800s continued to be an era of expanded travel with the development of the first steam locomotive to carry passengers and freight in 1825, the bicycle in 1876, the helicopter in 1877, the automobile in 1877, and the airplane in 1890.

The Time of the End

The year 1947 saw the first airplane exceed the speed of sound (742 mph). Nearly three decades later (1976), the United States Air Force set a world speed record that exceeded 2000 miles per hour (2,193 mph).[4] World leaders and businessmen can now sit across the table from one another within hours should the need arise.

In 1957, the Soviet Union launched the first satellite, Sputnik I. The U.S. Space Program (NASA) lifted off the ground during the sixties, sent men into orbit speeds of 20,000 mph, landed them on the moon, and brought them back safely. The space shuttle was launched in 1981 and became the first manned vehicle to enter and return from space intact. Certainly man can appropriately be described as "running to and fro" during this age of accelerated travel.

Rapid Communications. As with transportation, the field of communications has developed rapidly in recent times. Around 2000 B.C., the Egyptians were using a postal system for royal and administrative messages. Shortly after 1450 B.C., Moses used trumpets for assembling the people for "journeying of the camps," and to prepare for war. In 430 B.C., the Greeks used torches to send signals from hilltop to hilltop.

During the time of Christ, sending a letter from Jerusalem to Rome took several months: nearly 1900 years later, it still required about a year to send and receive a response halfway around the world. However, the field of communications quickly expanded with the development of the telegraph in 1837, the telephone in 1876, the radio in 1913 and the television in 1923.

Microwave technology, first developed for use with radar, began to be used for transmission of telephone conversations over land and greatly increased city-to-city communications. Coaxial cables increased the capacity of telephone lines, and the first transatlantic telephone cable was laid in 1956, making a telephone call between New York, Paris or London a common event. Multiple conference calls involving world leaders and international businesses have become routine with today's advanced technology.

Communications satellites, placed in geostationary orbits above the earth in the 1960s, made it possible to view events as they happened thousands of miles away. Weather satellites provide around-the-clock monitoring of hurricanes, tornadoes, floods, earthquakes and other potentially life-threatening events. Satellite transmission of military

Timeline 2000

action during the Persian Gulf War (1990-91) allowed the nations of the world to watch events unfold from their living room televisions.

In 1990, Voyager I took its final pictures of the sun and six of the planets from a distance of 3.7 billion miles from the earth. Transmission of the images to the earth through the solar system occurred at a speed of 600 million (600,000,000) miles per hour.

In July of 1997, the landing of a space craft (Pathfinder) on Mars with a small robot land rover (Sojourner) that analyzes the composition of rock and soil formations represented an amazing technological accomplishment for mankind. Transmission of pictures to the earth and communication of instructions to the two units were handled by NASA's Jet Propulsion Laboratory.

Pathfinder traveled at a speed of over 60,000 miles per hour to the red planet (309,000,000 miles, 211 days). Transmission of radio waves back to the earth from Sojourner took 10 minutes after traveling at a speed of nearly 2 billion miles/hour (1,854,000,000).

The Increase of Knowledge. In the past, it took hundreds of years for the total knowledge in the world to double. The early 20th century saw this time reduced to 10 years, and recently to less than 2 years. Daniel's prophecy that "knowledge would be increased" at the time of the end seems to be coming to pass in the midst of this knowledge explosion we are witnessing. Let's examine some of man's achievements and see just how far he has come.

Modern Warfare. For thousands of years, man fought with swords, bows and arrows, slingshots and spears. Crude contraptions by today's standards, such as battering rams and catapults were the ultimate in warfare. The discovery and use of gunpowder began an era which saw the first breech-loading rifle developed in 1811 and the machine gun in 1862. The 20th century brought submarines, bombers, helicopters, army tanks and aircraft carriers.

At the close of World War I, the first bomb was developed, and World War II unleashed the destructive power of the first atomic bomb. World War III, sure to come, will likely see the effects of the hydrogen bomb, the neutron bomb, and biological and germ warfare. The most recent phase of weapons deployment was efficiently demonstrated in the Persian Gulf War with laser-guided missiles.

Lasers have many applications today, including cutting tools in industry, surgery, bar code scanners and compact disc players. Military engineers envision using the laser to help destroy incoming missiles with highly concentrated bursts of light energy from strategically placed satellites high above the earth. Yesterday's science fiction has become today's reality!

New Technology. The business and scientific worlds have progressed from the simple adding machine to the complex computer. Up until the mid 1950s, electronic equipment operated with large, inefficient vacuum tubes. The invention of the transistor in 1947 changed all of that. By the latter part of the 1960s, the transistor had replaced practically all vacuum tubes in computers, televisions, radios and scientific instruments.

During the early 1970s, the first computer memory chips and microprocessors were introduced, making possible the use of microcomputers. The first personal home computers were introduced in the early 1980s. The rapid development of new technology in the 1990s makes computers purchased for homes and offices obsolete in just a few years.

Man can probe into the smallest parts of living matter with electron, scanning tunneling and atomic force microscopes and explore the outer realms of the universe with radio telescopes. The Hubble Space Telescope, producing images with 10 times the clarity of the best ground observatories, was launched in 1990. It became the principal instrument for exploring the universe during the next two decades.

The microtechnology that powered the U.S. space effort and led to the notebook computer is being surpassed by nanotechnology that manipulates individual atoms and molecules with parts thousands of times smaller than those used in conventional technology.

The Best Time to Live—The Worst Time to Live

The standard of living for many nations has increased significantly in this century due to improvements brought about by new technology. The rewards and benefits of a modern society, however, have not brought about advances in the social and moral standards of the world. Ironically, the world is abandoning the moral foundations and principles that have created the advanced society in which we live.

Basic standards of moral conduct set forth in the Bible, that are summarized in the Ten Commandments, are being discarded by those who have no respect for or fear of God (Romans 3:18). Rather than doing what is right, many are doing what is right in their own eyes

(Proverbs 21:2). Proverbs 3:7 tells us: *"Be not wise in thine own eyes: fear the Lord, and depart from evil."* God's judgment sooner or later falls upon those who refuse to obey the standards of righteousness taught in the Scriptures. *"Evil men understand not judgment: but they that seek the Lord understand all things"* (Proverbs 28:5).

Evil rulers bring a curse upon those over whom they rule. The writer of Proverbs said: *"When the righteous are in authority, the people rejoice: but when the wicked beareth rule, the people mourn"* (29:2). We may be living in "the best of times" today; however, if society continues down the road of decadence, we may soon be living in "the worst of times."

Perilous Times Will Come

The Bible informs us that in the days prior to the Lord's return, perilous times will come, and evil men will grow worse and worse, deceiving, and being deceived. Those who live Godly lives will suffer persecution (II Timothy 3:1-13). Spiritual darkness will settle over the world, and Godly discernment and understanding will be a rare commodity.

The prophet Daniel tells us that during this evil period: *"the people that do know their God shall be strong, and do exploits"* (Daniel 11:32). It will be an unprecedented opportunity to witness to those in spiritual darkness. *"And they that be wise shall shine as the brightness of the firmament; and they that turn many to righteousness as the stars for ever and ever"* (Daniel 12:3).

A Thief in the Night

If we are currently living in *"the time of the end"* as described in the Bible, we should be mindful of the apostle Peter's advice concerning the time of the Lord's return.

> *"Knowing this first, that there shall come in the last days scoffers, walking after their own lusts, and saying, Where is the promise of his coming?...The Lord is not slack concerning his promise, as some men count slackness; but is longsuffering to us-ward, not willing that any should perish, but that all should come to repentance.*
>
> *But the day of the Lord will come as a thief in the night; in the which the heavens shall pass away with a great noise, and the elements shall melt with fervent heat, the earth also and the works that are therein shall be burned up"* (II Peter 3:3-10).

Many Left Behind

The return of the Lord will find most people involved with the cares of this world and not watching for His return. They will be unprepared and will be left behind. Jesus Christ described the condition of the world when He returns for His own:

> *"And take heed to yourselves, lest at any time your hearts be overcharged with surfeiting, and drunkenness, and cares of this life, and so that day come upon you unawares. For as a snare shall it come on all them that dwell on the face of the whole earth. Watch ye therefore, and pray always, that ye may be accounted worthy to escape all these things that shall come to pass, and to stand before the Son of man"* (Luke 21: 34-36).

Watch and Be Prepared

In the Olivet Discourse, Christ gave several signs that would precede His return. After giving these signs to His disciples, He told them:

> *"…when these things begin to come to pass, then look up, and lift up your heads; for your redemption draweth nigh"* (Luke 21:28).

Many signs in the world today point to the soon return of Jesus Christ. It will be a joyous occasion for the believer and a terrifying experience for the unbeliever. Matthew Henry, respected Bible commentator from England during the 17th and 18th centuries, stated:

> "To watch implies not only to believe that our Lord will come, but to desire that He would come, to be often thinking of His coming, and always looking for it as sure and near, and the time of it uncertain." [5]

The evidence is overwhelming that we have entered an era in which man is running to and fro, and knowledge is increasing rapidly. Accelerated travel, rapid communications, the increase of knowledge, advances in modern warfare, new medical discoveries, and rapid changes in technology all point to a fulfillment of Daniel's prophecy during our generation.

Timeline 2000

If Daniel's prophecy is not in the process of fulfillment, what additional evidence should we look for? If the prophecy given by Daniel is a wake up call and warning to those living just prior to the Second Coming of Christ, what should be our response?

Charles H. Spurgeon, famous pastor of the Metropolitan Tabernacle in London, described the spiritual mindset that should be present in those who are seriously watching for the Lord's return.

> "While I am at work, my Master may come. Before I get weary, my Master may return. While others are mocking at me, my Master may appear; and whether they mock or applaud, is nothing to me, I live before the great Task-master's eye, and do my service knowing that He sees me, and expecting that by-and-by He will reveal Himself to me, and then He will reveal me and my right intention to misrepresenting men. May the Lord keep you waiting, working, watching…" [6]

— 10 —

SIGNS OF THE TIMES
Where Is Our Society Heading?

"Today we are facing a 'crisis of character' that is undermining every aspect of American life. This crisis is so severe that it amounts to a 'new cold war.' And the ethical and moral fallout threatens not only our political, economic, and intellectual well-being but our very 'destiny' as a nation…unless we wake up now and respond with moral conviction to these signs of the times, we face imminent and irreversible catastrophe." [1]

—D. James Kennedy

"When we forget that government is an institution of God and begin to allow evil to go unpunished, the entire government begins to break down…Ecclesiastes 8:11 says, 'Because sentence against an evil work is not executed speedily, therefore the heart of the sons of men is fully set in them to do evil.' If a speedy sentence is not brought about, men will do evil. And sentencing for crimes is not performed speedily at all in American society." [2]

—John MacArthur

The Removal of God from Society

Many social indicators reveal that we are living in a declining culture. The primary cause of this moral and spiritual decline has been the removal of God, the Bible and prayer from the public affairs of our nation, the schools and society. [3]

> "We see even our Supreme Court deciding that a man does not have to put his hand on the Bible as he takes an oath that he will support our Constitution, and that he will carry out his office." observes noted Bible scholar J. Vernon McGee. "They suppose that the Bible is not necessary because we no longer believe it is the Word of God. Other nations have gone down that repudiated God like that." [4]

The Bible tells us that *"God is love"* (I John 4:8), and that *"God so loved the world, that he gave his only begotten Son, that whosoever believeth in him should not perish, but have everlasting life"* (John 3:16). God's love is richly manifested to *"whosoever believeth in him"*! Psalm 84:11 and 12 reveal God's good intentions toward those who follow him:

> *"For the Lord God is a sun and shield: the Lord will give grace and glory: no good thing will he withhold from them that walk uprightly. O Lord of hosts, blessed is the man that trusteth in thee."*

Psalm 86:5 tells us that God wants us to follow Him: *"For thou, Lord, art good, and ready to forgive; and plenteous in mercy unto all them that call upon thee."* The Bible is full of Scriptures that express God's love towards mankind. Yet, even as a diamond has many facets, God's nature is not one-sided but multifaceted. The consequences of disobedience and rejection of God's love and plan of salvation bring judgment from a holy, just and righteous God who does not tolerate sin or allow it to go unpunished.

> "God has a permanent love for good and a permanent hatred of sin," says Theodore H. Epp. "There are those who think they can live in sin and still have the benefits of the love of God, but this is not scriptural. Because of God's love, He

provided His only begotten Son as a sacrifice for sin. Those who reject God's Son as their Saviour cannot expect the benefits of God's love." [5]

If your beliefs about God include only His love, mercy, forgiveness, rewards and benefits, you have not been properly introduced to the God of the Bible. God's love and mercy, as the Scriptures teach, are freely given to those who trust and follow in obedience. Those who do not follow God's commandments and teachings can expect only God's judgment and wrath in this life and the life to come.

"But be ye doers of the word, and not hearers only, deceiving your own selves" (James 1:22).

Woe unto the nation that forgets God's commandments! When a nation, city or community of people forget God and refuse to follow the commandments and precepts taught in the Bible and begin to engage in immoral and perverted lifestyles, God gives them over to corruption and certain destruction.

"God is jealous, and the Lord revengeth; the Lord revengeth, and is furious; the Lord will take vengeance on his adversaries, and he reserveth wrath for his enemies. The Lord is slow to anger, and great in power, and will not at all acquit the wicked: The Lord hath his way in the whirlwind (cyclones, hurricanes, tornadoes, typhoons) *and in the storm,* (rain, hail, high winds, floods) *and the clouds are the dust of his feet…The mountains quake* (earthquakes) *at him, and the hills melt* (volcanoes), *and the earth is burned* (fires, conflagration) *at his presence, yea, the world, and all that dwell therein. Who can stand before his indignation? and who can abide in the fierceness of his anger? his fury is poured out like fire, and the rocks are thrown down by him* (earthquakes). *The Lord is good, a strong hold in the day of trouble; and he knoweth them that trust him"* (Nahum 1: 2-7).

The Breakdown of Law and Order

The increasing tendency of those in positions of authority to do evil and call it good and attribute that which is good to being evil is becoming commonplace in society.

Contemporary Bible scholar Chuck Missler calls this conflict between good and evil a civil war.

> "The battle lines are drawn, the strategies are in place, the casualties are mounting. And the winner takes all," he says, pointing out that "God issued a severe warning to Israel in Isaiah 5:20: *'Woe unto them that call evil good, and good evil; that put darkness for light, and light for darkness; that put bitter for sweet, and sweet for bitter!'*…It appears that as a nation we have traveled the full spectrum from the loss of our Christian foundation to open rebellion against God's moral truth…"[6]

More and more frequently, high-level government officials are misleading and deceiving the public through carefully crafted statements that have subversive, hidden agendas. A lack of honesty and integrity in conducting the affairs of our nation and the absence of a high code of moral and ethical standards are having a devastating impact on the family.

The increasing violence in cities and communities and the lack of swift and certain justice in the courts have caused a breakdown of law and order that is permeating all levels of society. A contemptuous disregard of the Bible and an assault on the Ten Commandments by the judicial system of this country is a harbinger of future impending judgment from God.

Daniel Webster, who was born during the American Revolution and grew up listening to speeches of men like George Washington, John Adams, Thomas Jefferson, and James Madison, was a U. S. Senator and served as Secretary of State under three presidents.[7] Webster, a distinguished lawyer and defender of Christian teachings before the United States Supreme Court, stated:

> "…If we abide by the principles taught in the Bible, our country will go on prospering and to prosper; but if we and our posterity neglect its instructions and authority, no man can tell how sudden a catastrophe may overwhelm us and bury all our glory in profound obscurity."[8]

God allows people in positions of leadership to mislead, deceive, lie and do evil for a period of time; however, everything is being recorded in the books of heaven, and God will one day require those responsible to account for their actions.

> *"For the ways of man are before the eyes of the Lord, and he pondereth all his goings"* (Proverbs 5:21).
>
> *"For there is nothing covered, that shall not be revealed; neither hid, that shall not be known. Therefore whatsoever ye have spoken in darkness shall be heard in the light; and that which ye have spoken in the ear in closets shall be proclaimed upon the housetops. And I say unto you my friends, Be not afraid of them that kill the body, and after that have no more that they can do. But I will forewarn you whom ye shall fear: Fear him, which after he hath killed hath power to cast into hell; yea I say unto you, fear him"* (Luke 12:2-5).

The prophet Daniel gives us a glimpse of God's sovereign will over the nations of the earth and how He sometimes allows wicked rulers to come to power.

> *"…the most High ruleth in the kingdom of men, and giveth it to whomsoever he will, and setteth up over it the basest of men…And all the inhabitants of the earth are reputed as nothing: and he doeth according to his will in the army of heaven, and among the inhabitants of the earth: and none can stay his hand, or say unto him, What doest thou?…all whose works are truth, and his ways judgment: and those that walk in pride he is able to abase"* (Daniel 4:17,35,37).

As a large earthen or concrete dam slowly stores up a large reservoir of water, God's wrath is being stored up each day against public leaders who rule wickedly and trespass against Him. Psalms 7:11 says that *"God judgeth the righteous, and God is angry with the wicked every day."*

Although God is intentionally slow to anger, He does not allow sin to go unpunished. Every thought and action of every person on this planet will one day be accounted for and judged by a holy, just, all-knowing (omniscient), all-present (omnipresent) and all-powerful (omnipotent) God. Our works will be judged by fire. The believer's good works will be rewarded and the bad works will be destroyed.

The unbeliever will not have any good works according to God's standard of judgment. Nothing will be overlooked when the "Supreme Court of the Universe" meets at the Great White Throne Judgment (Rev. 20) to render the final verdict for all unbelievers.

The Breakdown of the Traditional Family

The decade of the "90s" has brought increased acceptance of socially immoral lifestyles and values that are condemned in the Holy Scriptures. According to Pastor Adrian Rogers, "Immorality has been the downfall of ancient Rome, ancient Greece, ancient Egypt, ancient Babylon and may well be the sin that destroys America." [9]

One of the most tragic casualties of this increase in immorality has been the breakdown of the family. Dr. Robert Lewis, a teaching pastor at a large metropolitan church in Little Rock, Arkansas, states:

> "Sometime in our recent past, American culture went from being a friend of the family to an adversary. Somehow, clear lines of right and wrong—of understanding what 'family values' means—were lost under the blanket of a 'do your own thing' mentality. Community values that once aligned with, reinforced, and supported marriage and family have all but evaporated." [10]

This rapid breakdown of the family structure and the decline of basic moral values have precipitated a scenario that resembles the discourse given by Timothy during the first century A.D.

> *"This know also, that in the last days perilous times shall come. For men shall be lovers of their own selves, covetous, boasters, proud, blasphemers, disobedient to parents, unthankful, unholy, without natural affection, trucebreakers, false accusers, incontinent, fierce, despisers of those that are good, traitors, heady, highminded, lovers of pleasures more than lovers of God; having a form of godliness, but denying the power thereof: from such turn away...ever learning, and never able to come to the knowledge of the truth...But evil men and seducers shall wax worse and worse, deceiving and being deceived"* (II Timothy 3:1-13).

Our society's move away from traditional family values "constitutes perhaps the greatest long-term threat to our children's well-being," says William J. Bennett, Secretary of Education under President Ronald Reagan. [11]

THE TWENTY-FIRST CENTURY
Will the Family Survive?

For the first time in the history of this nation, the institution of the family is being threatened by forces both within and outside the family structure. The family was first established by God when Adam and Eve were created, and Cain and Abel were born. Studies show that the basic family unit composed of a man, woman and children provides the best environment for the protection, nurturing and proper development of children. Gary Bauer, president of the Family Research Council in Washington, D.C., states:

> "Sadly, in the United States today, there's a flight from family responsibility, and the traditional family is increasingly in shambles…For the sake of the children, families must stay together, and they must teach their kids to respect authority." [12]

The Bible, an inexhaustible source of knowledge and wisdom for raising a family, teaches us how to raise children through proper discipline, exhortation, and instruction so that they will obey their parents, respect others and fear and honor God. John Quincy Adams, sixth president of the United States, said:

> "So great is my veneration for the Bible that the earlier my children begin to read it the more confident will be my hope that they will prove useful citizens of their country and respectable members of society. I have for many years made it a practice to read through the Bible once every year." [13]

Pastor Chuck Swindoll, of "Insight For Living" radio ministry, offers the following advice for those desiring to build strong families:

> "There is no school that families can attend and earn a degree in family strength. It doesn't work like that. Families

become strong, not because they have gone to a school and learned the rules, but because parents pay the price to be different...because they inculcate biblical truth in everyday life, conducting their relationships in the realm of wisdom, understanding, and knowledge." [14]

The Bible encourages us to teach our children to love God and follow His teachings and precepts:

> "And thou shalt love the Lord thy God with all thine heart, and with all thy soul, and with all thy might. And these words, which I command thee this day, shall be in thine heart: And thou shalt teach them diligently unto thy children, and shalt talk of them when thou sittest in thine house, and when thou walkest by the way, and when thou liest down, and when thou risest up" (Deuteronomy 6:5-7).

Families who read and study the Word of God together instill in their children an understanding of the values, morals and principles necessary to become productive members of society. Daniel Webster said:

> "If there is anything in my thoughts or style to commend, the credit is due to my parents for instilling in me an early love of the Scriptures." [15]

Dennis Rainey, Executive Director of FamilyLife Today headquartered in Little Rock, Arkansas tells families: "If you do not tackle your problems together with God's help, you will fall apart...If we wait until a crisis hits and then turn to the Scriptures, we won't be prepared..." [16]

In order to turn this nation around, we must begin to assume personal responsibility for the direction our family, city, state and country is headed and begin to look for ways to make a difference. We should not expect others to lead when we don't get personally involved in making changes at the local, state and national levels.

> "Every adult also has both the privilege and responsibility to influence local, state, and federal legislation that will dictate the environment in which a family lives," says George Barna of

Barna Research Group. "If more Christians let their elected officials know their feelings about such matters as divorce, abortion, child abuse, alimony, values clarification, public education, discipline, and litigation against parents, the law of the land would be quite different." Barna contends that "Lacking the input of people who believe in the worth of traditional families—in many cases, those who have wrongly assumed that their interests were being protected by elected officials—government has responded...to...people seeking to challenge bibically based values. The only way to protect the freedoms we possess and to restore some of those that have been removed is to get involved in the political process—through letters and calls to officials, by voting, attending town meetings, joining advocacy groups, and praying for God's blessing and direction in the political process." [17]

GOD CURSES THE NATION THAT FORGETS HIM!
Sliding Down a Slippery Slope

Our nation did not fall into a state of decadence overnight. This process has been going on for several decades, but God, who is merciful, has so far graciously refrained from harsh judgment of this nation. Perhaps the proclamation of the Gospel message around the world by evangelistic churches and ministries has been part of the reason God has withheld judgment. Many ministries in this country are providing salt and light (Matthew 5:13-16) to this nation and other parts of the world. Catastrophes in recent years due to unusual weather patterns and natural disasters may be warning signs that God's patience is wearing thin.

> "Unless we can get a firm grip on the ethical moorings of this country and stop its slide down the slippery slope of moral relativity and social decay, our entire culture will soon find itself on a high-speed ride to chaos and anarchy." [18]
>
> Pat Robertson

Actions and, in some cases, a lack of action on the part of the Executive, Legislative and Judicial branches of the United States have resulted in a progressive, incremental removal of the Bible, prayer and reverence for God from all aspects of society. We have sown the wind and we are beginning to reap the whirlwind (Hosea 8:7).

Our leaders need to reverse the foolish decisions that have corrupted our society and invite God back into the affairs of this nation! Surely those who will someday meet their Maker would rather hear the words *"Well done thou good and faithful servant..."* rather than *"...cast ye the unprofitable servant into outer darkness: there shall be weeping and gnashing of teeth"* (Matthew 25:21, 30).

God looks more favorably towards a nation and people that honor Him rather than a nation that refuses to acknowledge His presence. God doesn't need us, but we certainly need Him! Theologian R.C. Sproul points out:

> "To separate church and state is not to separate God and state. A state that refuses to acknowledge its subordination to God is on a collision course with the Lord of history."[19]

God's Recipe for National Repentance

In order to reverse the downward spiral into the pit of social immorality and decay, each of us must begin to take personal responsibility for the direction this nation is headed. We must elect leaders who have a proven track record of moral behavior, high ethical standards and integrity. What elected officials have done and what they are doing should carry more weight than what they say they are doing or tell us they are going to do. This may sound like a tall order, *"but with God, all things are possible"* (Matthew 19:26).

> "...I believe it is still possible for us to turn to God, and to grapple with many of our problems and begin to solve them," says evangelist Billy Graham. "We need responsible leaders from every area of life in the international arena—who have the dedication and the vision to provide moral and spiritual leadership for our generation." [20]

Such people of integrity may be rare, but "The Lord can give us men and women of character as He did so generously when the nation was young," says Dr. James C. Dobson, president of Focus on the Family, who urges Americans to "continue to ask God to restore the greatness of this country, and to give us leaders who will honor Him and live by the standards of righteousness." [21]

One way we can refocus our vision of where America should be going and embrace the principles and practices that made this country great is by taking a look at our past and by learning from those who helped found this nation. Benjamin Franklin eloquently summed up the respect and reverence for God and the Bible that prevailed during this country's infancy in his comments at the Constitutional Convention of 1787:

> "I have lived, Sir, a long time, and the longer I live the more convincing proofs I see of this truth: that God governs in the affairs of man. And if a sparrow cannot fall to the ground without His notice, is it probable that an empire can rise without His aid?
>
> We have been assured, Sir, in the Sacred Writings that except the Lord build the house, they labor in vain that build it. I firmly believe this…I therefore beg leave to move that, henceforth, prayers imploring the assistance of Heaven and its blessing on our deliberation be held in this assembly every morning before we proceed to business." [22]

Such respect and reverence for God and the Bible should be practiced at all levels in our society, and we should remove from office those who do not hold to such high standards of morality, ethics and integrity.

Finally, we need to turn to God and pray that he will restore our nation so that it will be a spiritual and moral lighthouse to the world as it was in years past. God's recipe for national repentance was given to Solomon, King of Israel, nearly three thousand years ago after completion of the temple.

> *"If my people, which are called by my name, shall humble themselves, and pray, and seek my face, and turn from their wicked ways; then will I hear from heaven, and will forgive their sin, and will heal their land"* (II Chronicles 7:14).

If our nation does not wake up and turn back to God, we will follow in the footsteps of other republics that have come and gone. Professor Alexander Tyler (1748-1813), while the thirteen colonies were still a part of England, wrote about the fall of the Athenian republic during the 4th century B.C.:

> "A democracy cannot exist as a permanent form of government. It can only exist until the voters discover that they can vote themselves money from the public treasure. From that moment on the majority always votes for the candidates promising the most money from the public treasury, with the result that a democracy always collapses over loose fiscal policy followed by a dictatorship. The average age of the world's great civilizations has been two hundred years. These nations have progressed through the following sequence: from bondage to spiritual faith, from spiritual faith to great courage, from courage to liberty, from liberty to abundance, from abundance to selfishness, from selfishness to complacency, from complacency to apathy, from apathy to dependency, from dependency back to bondage." [23]

The next few years will determine whether our nation turns around or continues down the path to destruction. If everyone will take personal responsibility to pray and get involved, God will do for this nation what He promised to do for King Solomon and the nation of Israel. If we wait for someone else to do what we need to do, the job won't get done! Edmund Burke (1729-1797), an English orator and statesman, said : "All that is necessary for the triumph of evil is that good men do nothing." [24]

If our nation does not begin turning back to the Biblical principles that made this country great, God will soon begin carving an epitaph on our nation's tombstone, like he did to the nation of Babylon over 2500 years ago when the mysterious handwriting appeared on the wall of the King's palace.

> *"God hath numbered thy kingdom, and finished it..Thou art weighed in the balances, and art found wanting..."* (Daniel 5:25-28).

That night, the King was slain and his kingdom was taken from him. When God numbers a kingdom and finishes it, it is all over. If our nation will turn back to God, there is still hope!

The prophet Jeremiah reveals God's course of action when a nation decides to go in the wrong direction:

> "*At what instant I shall speak concerning a nation, and concerning a kingdom, to pluck up, and to pull down, and to destroy it; If that nation, against whom I have pronounced, turn from their evil, I will repent of the evil that I thought to do unto them*" (Jeremiah 18:7,8).

We need to reevaluate our priorities and decide what is most important in this life for our families and for this great nation that God has raised up over the past two hundred years. Will we continue down the road of complacency, apathy and dependency and allow the forces that are destroying this nation to continue eating away at the traditional morals and values upon which this country was founded? Cal Thomas, a nationally syndicated columnist, tells us:

> "What we are as a country is determined in large measure by the way we were in the last generation. What we become will be determined by the choices we make now, in this generation…We can be an influence for evil, or an influence for good. It is our choice, and we have to select between those short-term, seemingly pleasurable experiences that promise everything but have brought near ruin to our nation—and the things that matter most." [25]

Will we behave like the proverbial frog that is slowly cooked in hot water because it doesn't detect the small incremental increases in temperature? Or will we wake up, take a stand and begin to make a difference in the direction this country is going? The decisions we make today will determine the course we will follow tomorrow!

> "The kind of society our children and our children's children will live in is at stake." says Donald E. Wildmon, Executive Director of the National Federation for Decency, "We can have a society that recognizes God and His moral standards, or we can have a godless society which recognizes the humanist religion with no absolute morals or values…The greatest tragedy is our refusal to get involved on behalf of those who will come after us. A nation which turns its back on God and His moral standards will reap what it sows. That was true 2,000 years ago. It is true today. It will be true 2,000 years from now…." [26]

— 11 —

WHAT IS YOUR SPIRITUAL TEMPERATURE?

"And I, brethren, could not speak unto you as unto spiritual, but as unto carnal, even as unto babes in Christ. I have fed you with milk, and not with meat: for hitherto ye were not able to bear it, neither yet now are ye able. For ye are yet carnal: for whereas there is among you envying, and strife, and divisions, are ye not carnal, and walk as men?"

—I Corinthians 3:1-3

"For the kingdom of heaven is as a man travelling into a far country, who called his own servants, and delivered unto them his goods…to every man according to his several ability…And so he that had received five talents came and brought other five talents, saying, Lord, thou deliveredst unto me five talents: behold, I have gained beside them five talents more. His lord said unto him, Well done, thou good and faithful servant: thou hast been faithful over a few things, I will make thee ruler over many things: enter thou into the joy of the lord."

—Matthew 25:14-21

Four Sobering Questions

Who am I? Where did I come from? What am I doing here? and *Where am I going when I die?* These important questions should be asked by every person at some point in his or her life.

People from different social, economic and ethnic backgrounds hold a wide variety of beliefs about God. In the final analysis, the only viewpoint that really matters is the one that is consistent with the Biblical account of God's character and attributes.

The question that should really be asked concerning man's existence on earth is not, *What does man think about God?* but rather, *What does God think about man?* Proverbs tells us: *"There is a way which seemeth right unto a man, but the end thereof are the ways of death"* (14:12).

When man tries to figure out God, he inevitably comes to the wrong conclusions. That is why it is important for each person to discover God's viewpoint, rather than depend upon their own limited thought and reasoning. God's viewpoint and plan for mankind is contained in the Bible.

> *"For my thoughts are not your thoughts, neither are your ways my ways, saith the Lord. For as the heavens are higher than the earth, so are my ways higher than your ways, and my thoughts than your thoughts"* (Isaiah 55:8,9).

The Natural Man

Discussing spiritual matters with a person who does not have spiritual perception is like discussing advanced math or science with someone who has never studied the basics in those subjects. Since spiritual understanding comes from God, man cannot fully comprehend God's Word or plan without a relationship with the Creator.

The Bible describes the spiritual man as one who has a personal relationship with God, and the natural man as one who does not know God personally and who cannot understand spiritual matters.

> *"Now we have received, not the spirit of the world, but the spirit of God; that we might know the things that are freely given to us of God. Which things also we speak, not in the words which man's wisdom teacheth, but which the Holy Ghost teacheth; comparing spiritual things with spiritual. But the natural man*

receiveth not the things of the Spirit of God: for they are foolishness unto him: neither can he know them, because they are spiritually discerned. But he that is spiritual judgeth all things, yet he himself is judged of no man. For who hath known the mind of the Lord, that he may instruct him? But we have the mind of Christ" (I Corinthians 2:12-16).

The Carnal Man

There are different levels of spiritual maturity in the body of Christ. The Scriptures draw a distinction between a spiritual believer and a carnal believer.

> *"And I, brethren, could not speak unto you as unto spiritual, but as unto carnal, even as unto babes in Christ. I have fed you with milk, and not with meat: for hitherto ye were not able to bear it, neither yet now are ye able. For ye are yet carnal: for whereas there is among you envying, and strife, and divisions, are ye not carnal, and walk as men?"* (I Corinthians 3:1-3).

Just as a young baby is unable to eat meat, a carnal Christian cannot receive spiritual meat. Rather, he must be fed basic spiritual food: the milk of the Word. A mature Christian will grow spiritually without having to be taught the basics over and over again. If a Christian is not growing and maturing in Christ, something is obviously wrong, and he should reevaluate his relationship with Christ.

> *"There is now no condemnation to them which are in Christ Jesus, who walk not after the flesh, but after the Spirit…For they that are after the flesh do mind the things of the flesh; but they that are after the Spirit the things of the Spirit. For to be carnally minded is death; but to be spiritually minded is life and peace.*
>
> *Because the carnal mind is enmity against God: for it is not subject to the law of God, neither indeed can be. So then they that are in the flesh cannot please God…But if the Spirit of him that raised up Jesus from the dead dwell in you, he that raised up Christ from the dead shall also quicken your mortal bodies by his Spirit that dwelleth in you…For if ye live after the flesh, ye shall die: but if ye through the Spirit do mortify the deeds of the body, ye shall live.*

For as many as are led by the Spirit of God, they are the sons of God…The Spirit itself beareth witness with our spirit, that we are the children of God: And if children, then heirs; heirs of God, and joint-heirs with Christ; if so be that we suffer with him, that we may be also glorified together" (Romans 8:1-17).

Spiritual Indicators

To grow spiritually, Christians must be open to changing those areas that are stunting their spiritual growth. A careful self-evaluation and diagnosis of one's spiritual condition may reveal spiritual problem areas.

Some questions to ask include: *How and where do I spend my time? How and where do I spend my money? What kind of television programs do I watch? What kind of programs and music do I listen to on the radio? What part of each day do I devote to prayer, Bible study and my relationship with God? Do I have any spiritual goals for my life?*

The answers to these questions reveal our true priorities and serve as spiritual indicators that reveal the level of our spiritual maturity in Christ. What we allow in and out of our minds and souls through the "eye gate," the "ear gate," and the "prayer gate" determines our spiritual relationship with God.

A Checkup From the Great Physician

"And Jesus answering said unto them, they that are whole need not a physician; but they that are sick. I came not to call the righteous, but sinners to repentance" (Luke 5:31-32).

A physical examination can reveal health problems that may not be detected from casual observation. If a health problem is detected soon enough, a person's life may be saved or prolonged.

Although the importance of our physical health seems obvious, we often overlook our spiritual health. Early detection of spiritual problems ensures a long, healthy and productive spiritual life with the fringe benefits that Heaven affords.

What is Your Spiritual Temperature?

The temperature of the human body when taken orally is around 98.6° F. Significant changes in the body's temperature reveal problems with our physical health. In a similar manner, our spiritual temperature (cold, lukewarm or hot) reveals our spiritual health.

A Spiritual Checklist

The book of Revelation describes three spiritual levels (hot, lukewarm and cold) in the passage addressed to the church of Laodicea:

> *"And unto the angel of the church of the Laodiceans write…I know thy works, that thou art neither cold nor hot: I would thou wert cold or hot. So then because thou art lukewarm, and neither cold nor hot, I will spue thee out of my mouth. Because thou sayest, I am rich, and increased with goods, and have need of nothing; and knowest not that thou are wretched, and miserable, and poor, and blind, and naked…As many as I love, I rebuke and chasten: be zealous therefore, and repent"* (Revelation 3:14-19).

A careful reading of this passage reveals that a lukewarm or cold spiritual condition is not acceptable to God. The person who is not a believer is considered spiritually dead. God wants our relationship with Him to be zealous (on fire or hot). Is your attitude, actions and relationship towards God hot, lukewarm or cold?

Rewards for Faithfulness

Man's accomplishments on earth are called "works" in the Bible. Good works will be rewarded, and bad works will be destroyed by fire, according to I Corinthians 3:11-17:

> *"For other foundation can no man lay than that is laid, which is Jesus Christ. Now if any man build upon this foundation gold, silver, precious stones, wood, hay, stubble; Every man's work shall be made manifest: for the day shall declare it, because it shall be revealed by fire; and the fire shall try every man's work of what sort it is.*
>
> *If any man's work abide which he hath built thereupon, he shall receive a reward. If any man's work shall be burned, he shall suffer loss: but he himself shall be saved; yet so as by fire. Know ye not that ye are the temple of God, and that the Spirit of God*

dwelleth in you? If any man defile the temple of God, him shall God destroy; for the temple of God is holy, which temple ye are."

The Spiritual Man

Those who lead spiritual lives will receive a greater reward than those who are carnal, whose works are mostly self-serving and will be destroyed by fire. Since the rewards given by God are eternal, we should take our service here on earth very seriously. In fact, the attitude believers should have towards God is summarized in II Peter 3: 11-18:

> *"Seeing then that all these things shall be dissolved, what manner of persons ought ye to be in all holy conversation and godliness, Looking for and hasting unto the coming of the day of God, wherein the heavens being on fire shall be dissolved, and the elements shall melt with fervent heat?*
>
> *Nevertheless we, according to his promise, look for new heavens and a new earth, wherein dwelleth righteousness. Wherefore, beloved, seeing that ye look for such things, be diligent that ye may be found of him in peace, without spot, and blameless.*
>
> *…Ye therefore, beloved, seeing ye know these things before, beware lest ye also, being led away with the error of the wicked, fall from your own stedfastness. But grow in grace, and in the knowledge of our Lord and Saviour Jesus Christ. To him be glory both now and for ever. Amen."*

The Uncertainty of Life

Everyone living today will someday die, unless the Lord intervenes, as He did with two select saints, Enoch and Elijah, in the Old Testament. The Bible tells us *"…it is appointed unto men once to die, but after this the judgment"* (Hebrews 9:27).

Death is not a pleasant subject; however, one day my name and yours will be listed among the many deceased in the obituaries of the daily newspaper. We don't know when that will be. We are all in a sense living on borrowed time. An accident or sickness may shorten our lifespan considerably. King Solomon, the wisest person who ever lived, said: *"Boast not thyself of tomorrow; for thou knowest not what a day may bring forth"* (Proverbs 27:1).

The question we should each ask ourselves is not; *When are we going to die?* but, *Where are we going when we die?* The uncertainty of life is discussed in the book of James:

"Go to now, ye that say, today or tomorrow we will go into such a city, and continue there a year, and buy and sell, and get gain: Whereas ye know not what shall be on the morrow, For what is your life? It is even a vapour, that appeareth for a little time, and then vanisheth away. For that ye ought to say, If the Lord will, we shall live, and do this, or that" (4:13-15).

The Brevity of Life

With an average lifespan of 70-80 years, man is here on earth for a very brief time. We should use that time wisely by arranging our thoughts, actions and priorities with an eye on eternity. Our priorities in life should be in order well before we are called to meet our Maker. The Bible describes one who had misplaced priorities and trusted in his riches rather than in God:

"Take heed, and beware of covetousness: for a man's life consisteth not in the abundance of the things which he possesseth. And he spake a parable unto them, saying, The ground of a certain rich man brought forth plentifully: And he thought within himself, saying, What shall I do, because I have no room where to bestow my fruits? And he said, This will I do: I will pull down my barns, and build greater; and there will I bestow all my fruits and goods. And I will say to my soul, Soul, thou hast much goods laid up for many years; take thine ease, eat, drink, and be merry. But God said unto him, Thou fool, this night thy soul shall be required of thee: then whose shall those things be, which thou hast provided? So is he that layeth up treasure for himself, and is not rich toward God" (Luke 12: 15-21).

The Value of a Soul

The most important decision you will ever make in this life is to put God first in your life. Don't put it off! Jesus told His disciples that there is nothing in this world more valuable than your soul. In fact, all the riches in the world, if they could be obtained, will do you no good after you die.

"...Whosoever will come after me, let him deny himself, and take up his cross, and follow me. For whosoever will save his life shall lose it; but whosoever shall lose his life for my sake and the gospel's, the same shall save it. For what shall it profit a man, if he shall gain the whole world, and lose his own soul? Or what shall a man give in exchange for his soul?" (Mark 8:34-37).

A Certain Appointment with God

"Look unto me, and be ye saved, all the ends of the earth: for I am God, and there is none else. I have sworn by myself, the word is gone out of my mouth in righteousness, and shall not return, That unto me every knee shall bow, every tongue shall swear" (Isaiah 45:22,23).

When a certain lawyer asked Jesus *"Master, what shall I do to inherit eternal life?"* he was told to do the following and he would live: *"Thou shalt love the Lord thy God with all thy heart, and with all thy soul, and with all thy strength, and with all thy mind: and thy neighbor as thyself"* (Luke 10:25-28).

In whom or what are you trusting today? Have you put God first? Don't postpone the most important decision in your life! Your next opportunity to be saved and go to Heaven is today! *"Behold, now is the accepted time; behold now is the day of salvation"* (II Corinthians 6:2). Your response to God's Word will help you evaluate your spiritual temperature and determine whether your thoughts and actions are leading you toward God (hot) or away from God (cold).

— 12 —

THE GREAT ESCAPE!

"The wicked shall be turned into hell and all the nations that forget God."

—Psalms 9:17

"For if they escaped not who refused him that spake on earth, much more shall not we escape, if we turn away from him that speaketh from heaven…Wherefore…let us have grace, whereby we may serve God acceptably with reverence and godly fear: For our God is a consuming fire."

—Hebrews 12:25-29

"The way of life is above to the wise, that he may depart from hell beneath".

—Proverbs 15:24

The Terror of the Lord

"…*For we must all appear before the judgment seat of Christ; that everyone may receive the things done in his body, according to that he hath done, whether it be good or bad. Knowing therefore the terror of the Lord, we persuade men…*" (II Corinthians 5:10,11).

Why would someone like the Apostle Paul devote his entire life to trying to persuade men to turn from their sinful ways and trust in the Lord? The answer Paul gave reveals the severity of not following God's way: *"Knowing therefore the terror of the Lord, we persuade men..."* The book of Jude (21-23) warns us: *"Keep yourselves in the love of God, looking for the mercy of our Lord Jesus Christ unto eternal life...And others save with fear, pulling them out of the fire..."*

The spiritually blind condition described in the book of Revelation is prevalent among many of the religious people in the world today.

> *"Because thou sayest, I am rich, and increased with goods, and have need of nothing; and knowest not that thou are wretched, and miserable, and poor, and blind, and naked..."* (Revelation 3:17)

Many have become so comfortable in their lifestyles that they are blind to their spiritual condition and their future appointment with God. Simply put: There is no fear of God in their eyes!

The Bible is frank in its assessment of mankind: *"Evil men understand not judgment: but they that seek the Lord understand all things."* (Proverbs 28:5) Those who have no interest in following the Lord do not realize the serious consequences of their decision and actions. As someone said: Eternity is far too long to be wrong!

Why Should I Fear a Loving God?

It is not popular today to talk about the judgment of God. The love of God is a much more popular topic and evokes little criticism. The topics of sin, hell, judgment and the fear of God are ignored and avoided by many ministers and teachers in order not to offend or make others feel uncomfortable. Those who avoid teaching and preaching the whole counsel of God are more interested in pleasing men rather than God. The Apostle Paul in his later years stated:

> *"And now, behold, I know that ye all, among whom I have gone preaching the kingdom of God, shall see my face no more. Wherefore I take you to record this day, that I am pure from the blood of all men. For I have not shunned to declare unto you all the counsel of God. Take heed therefore unto yourselves, and to all the flock, over the which the Holy Ghost hath made you overseers,*

to feed the church of God, which he hath purchased with his own blood" (Acts 20:25-28).

Although men may dilute and change God's message, His Word does not change, and all 66 books of the Bible are just as relevant to the problems and issues we face today as they were in previous generations. *"For I am the Lord, I change not..."* (Malachi 3:6). Our lives may sometimes be inconsistent and unstable; however, God will always be reliable and dependable. *"Jesus Christ the same yesterday, and today and forever"* (Hebrews 13:8).

The Bible has a lot to say about God's love to those who are following Him. The Bible is also very clear concerning the consequences of not following God, and tells us to warn those who refuse to obey. The prophet Ezekiel was told to warn both the righteous and the wicked to turn from their ways.

> *"When I say unto the wicked, Thou shalt surely die; and thou givest him not warning, nor speakest to warn the wicked from his wicked way, to save his life; the same wicked man shall die in his iniquity; but his blood will I require at thine hand. Yet if thou warn the wicked, and he turn not from his wickedness, nor from his wicked way, he shall die in his iniquity; but thou hast delivered thy soul.*
>
> *Again, When a righteous man doth turn from his righteousness, and commit iniquity, and I lay a stumblingblock before him, he shall die: because thou hast not given him warning, he shall die in his sin, and his righteousness which he hath done shall not be remembered; but his blood will I require at thine hand. Nevertheless if thou warn the righteous man, that the righteous sin not, and he doth not sin, he shall surely live, because he is warned; also thou hast delivered thy soul"* (Ezekiel 3:18-21).

Advice From a Wise Man

The wisest man who ever lived, Solomon, after experiencing many of the pleasures and rewards of this life, concluded that life was vanity and man should:

> *"Fear God, and keep his commandments: for this is the whole duty of man. For God shall bring every work into judgment, with*

every secret thing, whether it be good, or whether it be evil" (Ecclesiastes 12:13,14).

If Solomon, with all his wisdom, concluded that we should *"Fear God, and keep his commandments,"* what conclusion should each of us draw? Jesus Christ, who was greater than Solomon (Matt. 12:42), taught His disciples the fear of God.

> *"And I say unto you my friends, Be not afraid of them that kill the body, and after that have no more that they can do. But I will forewarn you whom ye shall fear: Fear him, which after he hath killed hath power to cast into hell; yea, I say unto you, Fear him..."* (Luke 12:4,5).

Many Scriptures in the Bible warn those who refuse to follow God of the price for rebellion and disobedience. The short-term comforts and pleasures of sin in this world should be rejected if they are hindering our relationship with God.

> *"For if we sin wilfully after that we have received the knowledge of the truth, there remaineth no more sacrifice for sins, But a certain fearful looking for of judgment and fiery indignation which shall devour the adversaries...And again, The Lord shall judge his people. It is a fearful thing to fall into the hands of the living God"* (Hebrews 10:26-31).

The Rich Man and Lazarus

The book of Luke describes the "horrors of hell" that awaited a rich man who chose life's temporary pleasures rather than God's way. Those who are following the broad way that leads to destruction rather than the narrow way that leads to eternal life should ponder the consequences of experiencing God's wrath in hell rather than God's love in heaven.

> *"There was a certain rich man, which was clothed in purple and fine linen, and fared sumptuously every day: And there was a certain beggar named Lazarus, which was laid at his gate, full of sores, And desiring to be fed with the crumbs which fell from the rich man's table: moreover the dogs came and licked his sores.*

The Great Escape

> *And it came to pass, that the beggar died, and was carried by the angels into Abraham's bosom: the rich man also died, and was buried; And in hell he lift up his eyes, being in torments, and seeth Abraham afar off, and Lazarus in his bosom. And he cried and said, Father Abraham, have mercy on me, and send Lazarus, that he may dip the tip of his finger in water, and cool my tongue; for I am tormented in this flame.*
>
> *But Abraham said, Son, remember that thou in thy lifetime receivedst thy good things, and likewise Lazarus evil things: but now he is comforted, and thou are tormented. And beside all this, between us and you there is a great gulf fixed: so that they which would pass from hence to you cannot; neither can they pass to us, that would come from thence.*
>
> *Then he said, I pray thee therefore, father, that thou wouldest send him to my father's house: For I have five brethren; that he may testify unto them, lest they also come into this place of torment. Abraham saith unto him, They have Moses and the prophets; let them hear them. And he said, Nay, father Abraham: but if one went unto them from the dead, they will repent. And he said unto him, If they hear not Moses and the prophets, neither will they be persuaded, though one rose from the dead"* (Luke 16:19-31).

The Bible contains all the essential information one needs to avoid spending an eternity in hell. Taking a chance and hoping that hell does not exist is the worst decision one can make in this life. An eternity of regret in hell cannot compare with an eternity of rejoicing that awaits the believer in heaven.

THE GREAT ESCAPE!

What is "The Great Escape"? The "Great Escape" is not an escape from prison or from any other type of confinement here on earth. The "Great Escape" is not an escape from our problems or the horrible circumstances we sometimes encounter. The "Great Escape" is not an escape from physical death. The "Great Escape" is an escape from spiritual death (the second death) and eternal separation from God. [1]

The Bible describes two births (physical and spiritual) and two deaths (physical and spiritual). Mankind easily understands the physical birth and death of a person. But the concept of spiritual birth and death is a bit more difficult to grasp. Spiritual birth, being born again, takes place when one trusts in Jesus Christ for salvation and is remade alive spiritually by the Holy Spirit. Spiritual death occurs when all unbelievers are judged at the Great White Throne Judgment and are cast into the lake of fire. Blessed is the person who is born twice and dies once! Cursed is the person who is born once and dies twice!

The Great White Throne Judgment

All unbelievers will one day kneel before the "Supreme Court of the Universe" and be sentenced to eternal damnation and separation from God. Those whose names are not written in the book of life will be thrown into the lake of fire. If you do not trust in Jesus Christ as your Saviour, your name will not be found in the Book of Life on the day of judgment.

If you end up at the Great White Throne Judgment, your fate will have already been sealed. It will be too late for you to change your eternal destiny. Now is the time for you to escape the Great White Throne Judgment. In order to be part of "The Great Escape," your name must be recorded in the Book of Life. Is your name there?

> *"And I saw a great white throne, and him that sat on it, from whose face the earth and the heaven fled away; and there was found no place for them. And I saw the dead, small and great, stand before God; and the books were opened: and another book was opened, which is the book of life: and the dead were judged out of those things which were written in the books, according to their works.*
>
> *And the sea gave up the dead which were in it; and death and hell delivered up the dead which were in them: and they were judged every man according to their works. And death and hell were cast into the lake of fire. This is the second death. And whosoever was not found written in the book of life was cast into the lake of fire"* (Revelation 20:11-15).

What is Keeping You out of Heaven?

Most people say they want to go to Heaven and believe that is where they will end up after death, but few people actually do what is necessary to go there. What is preventing you from receiving eternal life and the rewards, riches and pleasures of Heaven?

> *"Enter ye in at the strait gate: for wide is the gate, and broad is the way, that leadeth to destruction, and many there be which go in thereat: Because strait is the gate, and narrow is the way, which leadeth unto life, and few there be that find it"* (Matthew 7:13-14).

Has pride in your physical appearance, accomplishments, possessions, wealth or status in life blinded you to the importance of your relationship with God? What stumbling block is keeping you out of heaven? Jesus used some illustrations that seem strange, but are very practical and straightforward concerning the choices we make in this life.

> *"…if thy hand offend thee, cut it off: it is better for thee to enter into life maimed, than having two hands to go into hell, into the fire that never shall be quenched: Where their worm dieth not, and the fire is not quenched. And if thy foot offend thee, cut it off: it is better for thee to enter halt into life, than having two feet to be cast into hell, into the fire that never shall be quenched: Where their worm dieth not, and the fire is not quenched. And if thine eye offend thee, pluck it out: it is better for thee to enter into the kingdom of God with one eye, than having two eyes to be cast into hell fire: Where their worm dieth not, and the fire is not quenched"* (Mark 9:43-48).

Although the sins and transgressions committed in this life will be convicting evidence on the day of judgment, good works and good deeds are not sufficient to get you into heaven. Only God's forgiveness can cancel the consequences of past and future sin in your life.

> *"Not every one that saith unto me, Lord, Lord, shall enter into the kingdom of heaven; but he that doeth the will of my Father which is in heaven. Many will say to me in that day, Lord, Lord, have we not prophesied in thy name? and in thy name have cast out devils? and in thy name done many wonderful works? And then will I profess unto them, I never knew you: depart from me, ye that work iniquity"* (Matthew 7: 21-23).

Don't Miss the Boat!

Many of life's most important decisions involve two choices: Will I follow God's way or my way? God told Moses and the children of Israel to choose between life and death, good and evil.

> "... I have set before thee this day life and good, and death and evil; In that I command thee this day to love the Lord thy God, to walk in his ways, and to keep his commandments and his statutes and his judgments, that thou mayest live and multiply: and the Lord thy God shall bless thee in the land whither thou goest to possess it.
>
> But if thine heart turn away, so that thou wilt not hear, but shalt be drawn away, and worship other gods, and serve them; I denounce unto you this day, that ye shall surely perish, and that ye shall not prolong your days upon the land...I call heaven and earth to record this day against you, that I have set before you life and death, blessing and cursing: therefore choose life, that both thou and thy seed may live:
>
> That thou mayest love the Lord thy God, and that thou mayest obey his voice, and that thou mayest cleave unto him: for he is thy life, and the length of thy days..." (Deuteronomy 30:15-20).

Joshua, who succeeded Moses as leader of the tribes of Israel, told the people to "...*fear the Lord, and serve him in sincerity and in truth...and if it seem evil unto you to serve the Lord, choose you this day whom ye will serve...but as for me and my house, we will serve the Lord*" (Joshua 24:14-15).

Don't Give Up!

Dr. Tony Evans, pastor and Bible scholar, tells us to "run the race" without giving up.

"If you are not dead yet, you are not finished yet," he says. "You still have time to get in the race! You may be coming to the starting blocks with regrets over personal, family, or spiritual failure...You may even be starting the race a little late, but God can help you make up for lost time." Evans cites the apostle Paul's persistence: "*He forgot the things that were behind him. His eyes were straight ahead, focused on the prize*" (Philippians 3:13-14).

Encouraging his listeners to avoid distractions and to claim His grace, Evans concludes that: "There is only one passion in life worth your total pursuit. And that is to love and serve Christ in such a way that you win the race and receive His approval…Jesus Christ said, *'I am the Alpha and the Omega, the First and the Last, the Beginning and the End.'* (Revelation 22:13) …Whatever your need may be, whatever may be dragging you down, if it fits between those two extremes, Jesus Christ can do something about it. So you have nothing to lose by going for the Prize!" [2]

Which way have you chosen? God's way or your way? Life and good or death and evil? Choose life and live eternally! Choose death, and you will perish eternally! Choose life, and Heaven will be your reward!

HOW TO BE SURE YOU ARE GOING TO HEAVEN!

1) You must recognize you are a sinner.

"All we like sheep have gone astray; we have turned every one to his own way…" (Isaiah 53:6).

"The fool hath said in his heart, There is no God. They are corrupt, they have done abominable works, there is none that doeth good. The Lord looked down from heaven upon the children of men, to see if there were any that did understand, and seek God. They are all gone aside, they are all together become filthy: there is none that doeth good, no, not one" (Psalm 14: 1-3).

"As it is written, There is none righteous, no, not one: There is none that understandeth, there is none that seeketh after God. They are all gone out of the way, they are together become unprofitable; there is none that doeth good, no, not one…Their feet are swift to shed blood: Destruction and misery are in their ways: And the way of peace have they not known: There is no fear of God before their eyes…For all have sinned and come short of the glory of God" (Romans 3: 10-18, 23).

Only one sin is necessary to qualify as a sinner. Start guessing if you are not sure. If you have a problem admitting you are a sinner in need of a Savior, your own personal pride and ego has blinded you spiritually and built a barrier or wall that prevents you from seeing yourself as God sees you and keeps you from having a saving relationship with God.

2) You must realize you need a Savior.

> "Wherefore as by one man sin entered into the world, and death by sin; and so death passed upon all men, for that all have sinned: (For until the law sin was in the world: but sin is not impuuted when there is no law. Nevertheless death reigned from Adam to Moses, even over them that had not sinned after the similitude of Adam's transgression, who is the figure of him that was to come. But not as the offence, so also is the free gift.
> For if through the offence of one many be dead, much more the grace of God, and the gift by grace, which is by one man, Jesus Christ, hath abounded unto many. And not as it was by one that sinned, so is the gift: for the judgment was by one to condemnation, but the free gift is of many offences unto justification.
> For if by one man's offence death reigned by one; much more they which receive abundance of grace and of the gift of righteousness shall reign in life by one, Jesus Christ.) Therefore as by the offence of one judgment came upon all men to condemnation; even so by the righteousness of one the free gift came upon all men unto justification of life. For as by one man's disobedience many were made sinners, so by the obedience of one shall many be made righteous" (Romans 5: 12-19).
>
> "For when we were yet without strength, in due time Christ died for the ungodly. For scarcely for a righteous man will one die: yet peradventure for a good man some would even dare to die. But God commendeth his love toward us, in that, while we were yet sinners, Christ died for us. Much more then, being now justified by his blood, we shall be saved from wrath through him. For if when we were enemies, we were reconciled to God by the death of his Son, much more, being reconciled, we shall be saved by his life...For the wages of sin is death; but the gift of God is eternal life through Jesus Christ our Lord" (Romans 5: 6-10, 6: 23).

Jesus Christ, through His death on the cross, has provided the only way to get to Heaven. As Peter stated in Acts 4:12: "Neither is there salvation in any other: for there is none other name under heaven given among men, whereby we must be saved."

An open invitation has been extended to enter the door that leads to eternal life.

> *"Behold, I stand at the door, and knock: if any man hear my voice, and open the door, I will come in to him, and will sup with him, and he with me. To him that overcometh will I grant to sit with me in my throne, even as I also overcame, and am set down with my Father in his throne"* (Revelation 3: 20-21).

If you want to go to heaven, you must go through the Door. There is no other way! *"Jesus saith unto him, I am the way, the truth, and the life: no man cometh unto the Father, but by me"* (John 14:6).

3) You must be willing to change your lifestyle and way of thinking.

> *"Therefore if any man be in Christ, he is a new creature: old things are passed away; behold, all things are become new"* (II Corinthians 5:17).

Your thoughts, actions and behaviors will change as God works in your life. This turning from your former lifestyle is called repentance. Repentance is more than feeling sorry for your sins. Godly repentance involves changing the direction you are going (away from God) and committing your life to following God's plan and purpose. *"But be ye doers of the word, and not hearers only, deceiving your own selves"* (James 1:22).

If you do not see evidence of changes in your way of thinking, your lifestyle and your relationship with God and other people, you need to reexamine your salvation experience and relationship with God.

> *"Jesus answered and said unto him, If a man love me, he will keep my words: and my Father will love him, and we will come unto him, and make our abode with him. He that loveth me not keepeth not my sayings: and the word which ye hear is not mine, but the Father's which sent me"* (John 14: 23-24).
>
> *"Love not the world, neither the things that are in the world. If any man love the world, the love of the Father is not in him. For all that is in the world, the lust of the flesh, and the lust of the eyes, and the pride of life, is not of the Father, but is of the world. And the world passeth away, and the lust thereof: but he that doeth the will of God abideth for ever"* (I John 2: 15-17).

"Be not deceived; God is not mocked: for whatsoever a man soweth, that shall he also reap. For he that soweth to his flesh shall of the flesh reap corruption; but he that soweth to the Spirit shall of the Spirit reap life everlasting. And let us not be weary in well doing: for in due season we shall reap, if we faint not. As we have therefore opportunity, let us do good unto all men, especially unto them who are of the household of faith" (Galations 6:7-10).

4) **You must ask God to forgive you for the sins you have committed against Him and ask Him to come in and take control of your life.**

"Trust in the Lord with all thine heart; and lean not unto thine own understanding. In all thy ways acknowledge him, and he shall direct thy paths. Be not wise in thine own eyes: fear the Lord, and depart from evil" (Proverbs 3: 5-7).

"For God so loved the world that he gave his only begotten Son, that whosoever believeth in him should not perish, but have everlasting life. For God sent not his Son into the world to condemmn the world; but that the world through him might be saved. He that believeth on him is not condemned: but he that believeth not is condemned already, because he hath not believed in the name of the only begotten Son of God" (John 3:16-18).

5) **Thank God for saving you and making you a new creation through Jesus Christ's sacrifice on the cross and atonement for your sins so that you might inherit eternal life and escape the eternal punishment and damnation of Hell.**

"For by grace are ye saved through faith; and that not of yourselves: it is the gift of God: Not of works, lest any man should boast" (Ephesians 2:8,9).

"There is therefore now no condemnation to them which are in Christ Jesus, who walk not after the flesh, but after the Spirit" (Romans 8:1).

If you have truly trusted in Jesus Christ as your personal Savior, please sign your name and date as a witness to heaven, yourself and others of your decision.

_____   _____
Name   Date

If you have received Jesus Christ as your Savior, you can rejoice as John Newton (1725-1807) when he wrote the classic hymn "Amazing Grace."

> Amazing grace how sweet the sound
> That saved a wretch like me!
> I once was lost but now am found
> Was blind but now I see
>
> Twas grace that taught my heart to fear,
> And grace my fears relieved;
> How precious did that grace appear
> The hour I first believed!
>
> Through many dangers, toils and snares
> I have already come;
> Tis grace hath brought me safe thus far
> And grace will lead me home.
>
> When we've been there ten thousand years,
> Bright shining as the sun,
> We've no less days to sing God's praise
> Than when we first begun.

6) **Begin to communicate with God often through prayer; study the Bible regularly; attend a Bible-teaching church; be baptised as soon as possible; and look for ways to grow spiritually and strengthen your faith so that you can help others find God's saving grace.**

Concluding Thoughts

I hope this book has challenged you, the reader, to look at your own relationship with God, evaluate your spiritual condition in the light of the Bible, establish God as the top priority in your life and live the remaining years of your life in service to the Almighty, Holy, Sovereign God of the Universe who rules over both time and eternity.

As the Psalmist said: *"The heavens declare the glory of God; and the firmament* (earth) *sheweth his handywork"* (19:1). God's design in creation is clearly and unmistakably revealed to those who are looking for it (Romans 1:18-32). The Creator has also revealed His presence while guiding and preserving the children of Israel down through the 4000 year timeline that is presented on the back cover. God has majestically and wonderfully woven His thread of sovereignty into the tapestry of Jewish history.

This is the most exciting time in history for the believer to be living. The return of the Jews to Palestine during this century as predicted in the Bible and the many converging Bible prophecies that are coming together before our very eyes strongly indicate that we are living during *the time of the end* as described by the Prophet Daniel.

As the end-time scenario draws closer and comes more clearly into focus, the prominent characters in Israel and the Mideast will be lining up on stage for the final drama of the current age. The events that will take place prior to the Second Coming of Christ are described in the Olivet Discourse, given by Jesus Christ nearly 2000 years ago. (Matthew 24, Mark 13, Luke 21) Jesus told His disciples:

> *"...when these things begin to come to pass, then look up, and lift up your heads; for your redemption draweth nigh"* (Luke 21:28).

Jesus predicted that many will be caught off-guard. *"For as a snare shall it come on all them that dwell on the face of the whole earth"* (Luke 21:35). Jesus' advice to the generation that would be living prior to His return was to *"Watch ye therefore, and pray always, that ye may be accounted worthy to escape all these things that shall come to pass, and to stand before the Son of man"* (21:36).

Jesus Told Us to Watch, Pray and Be Prepared!

"But of that day and hour knoweth no man, no, not the

angels of heaven, but my Father only…watch therefore: for ye know not what hour your Lord doth come. But know this, that if the goodman of the house had known in what watch the thief would come, he would have watched, and would not have suffered his house to be broken up.

> *Therefore*
> *be ye also ready:*
> *for in such an hour as ye think not*
> *the Son of man cometh."*
> Matthew 24:36-44

Are You Ready?

Appendix A

Problems with Hebrew Chronology

Dr. Thiele summarized some of the problems encountered with establishing accurate dates for Old Testament events.

"For more than two thousand years, Hebrew chronology has been a serious problem for Old Testament scholars. Every effort to weave the chronological data of the kings of Israel and Judah into some sort of harmonious scheme seemed doomed to failure...The greatest drawback in the study of Old Testament chronology has been, and still remains, a tendency to hold to certain preconceived opinions without first endeavoring to ascertain just what the Hebrews did in the matter of chronological procedure.

"Altogether too often we formulate our own conclusions as to what they did, or should have done. Then, without sufficient evidence, we endeavor to produce chronological schemes in accord with our own predetermined ideas, only to be led into impossible impasses and hopeless confusion...We must approach the work of the ancient Hebrew chronologists with an open mind, examining fairly and objectively what they did, and, on the basis of facts, build our interpretation of the data they have left for us.

"The only basis for a sound chronology of the period to be discussed is a completely unbiased use of the biblical statements in the light of all other knowledge we can bring to bear on this problem, notably the history and chronology of the ancient Near East."

Edwin R. Thiele
February 7, 1951

The Mysterious Numbers of the Hebrew Kings, Edwin R. Thiele, Grand Rapids, Michigan: Zondervan Publishing Company, 1983, 15, 16

Twenty Years Later

In 1963, more than twenty years after his initial work on the chronology of the Hebrew kings was introduced, Dr. Thiele commented on his findings.

"More and more my chronological pattern of Hebrew history is finding acceptance, in whole or in part, in the scholarly world. Criticisms fall into two main categories. On the one hand, certain members of liberal groups do not regard it possible for these numbers to have been handed down through so many years and so many hands "without often becoming corrupt." On the other, a few vigorously outspoken members of conservative groups view with horror any questions that may be raised concerning the absolute accuracy of any details in the Old Testament chronological data...

Scholars impelled solely by a sincere desire for truth and an earnest effort to find it, and religious believers who find in God the very embodiment of truth and in the Hebrew Scriptures its most absolute expression, find little difficulty in putting aside early notions and accepting new light whenever and however it may come."

Edwin R. Thiele
September 1963

The Mysterious Numbers of the Hebrew Kings, Edwin R. Thiele, Grand Rapids, Michigan: Zondervan Publishing Company, 1983, 20

Thirty Years Later

In April of 1982, Dr. Thiele's preface to a third edition stated:

"Thirty years after the publication of my solution to the problem of the mysterious numbers of the Hebrew kings comes a need for a new edition. Confused and erroneous though these numbers appeared to be, they have proven themselves to be remarkably accurate...It is my hope that this presentation will serve to bring confidence in the biblical numbers of the Hebrew kings, in the God who placed them on their thrones, and in the principles of righteousness He expected them to uphold. This confidence, now so woefully lacking, is our primary need

Appendix A

in our troubled and perplexed times. If we would restore confidence in God, we must restore confidence in the Bible—confidence that comes through an intelligent trust."

Edwin R. Thiele
April, 1982

The Mysterious Numbers of the Hebrew Kings, Edwin R. Thiele, Grand Rapids, Michigan: Zondervan Publishing Company, 1983, 23, 24

Fifty Years Later

Since the original publication of Dr. Thiele's studies in 1944, his writings have been accepted by many academic institutions and scholars around the world. Thiele's chronology has maintained its position in the academic world for over fifty years. A representative of Paternoster Press in Britain called Thiele's work "the basis of all subsequent investigation in this field, and the standard authority on the subject."

Archaeology and Bible History, Joseph P. Free, Howard F. Vos, Grand Rapids, Michigan: Zondervan Publishing House, 1992, 151

Additional Supporting Sources

The *Cambridge Ancient History* adopted Thiele's chronology which placed Solomon's death at 931 B.C. Thiele's chronology has been adopted by many seminary professors including Dr. Eugene H. Merrill, who holds a Ph.D. from Columbia University and is Professor of Semitics and Old Testament studies at Dallas Theological Seminary.

Dr. Gleason L. Archer (B.A., M.A., Ph.D., Harvard University; B.D., Princeton Theological Seminary; L.L.B., Suffolk Law School) professor of Old Testament at Trinity Evangelical Divinity School, Deerfield, Illinois, and Dr. Leon J. Wood (1918-1977), (Ph.D., Michigan State University), former Professor of Old Testament Studies and Dean of the Grand Rapids Baptist Seminary, reference Dr. Edwin R. Thiele's chronological dating system as contained in *The Mysterious Numbers of the Hebrew Kings.*

Kingdom of Priests, Eugene H. Merrill, Grand Rapids, Michigan: Baker Book House Company, 67

A Survey of Old Testament Introduction, Gleason L. Archer, Moody Bible Institute, Moody Press, 1964, 1974, 229

A Survey of Israel's History, Leon J. Wood, Grand Rapids, Michigan: Zondervan Publishing House, Academie Books, 386

Appendix B

The date of 931-930 B.C. is commonly used for the date of Solomon's death and the division of the Kingdom. Older books use a date forty to fifty years earlier for the death of Solomon, however "All books written in the light of recent discoveries date Solomon's death in the 930s B.C." Mowinckel, Maisler, and Yelvin date Solomon's death at 930 B.C.; Aharoni and Tadmor at 928 B.C.

Archaeology and Bible History, Joseph P. Free, Howard F. Vos, Grand Rapids, Michigan: Zondervan Publishing House, 1992, 149

Appendix C

THE REIGNS OF JEROBOAM AND REHOBOAM

AUTHOR	DATE OF PROPOSAL	KING OF ISRAEL Jeroboam I	KING OF JUDAH Rehoboam
Albright (1891-1971)	1970 A.D.	922-901 B.C.	922-915 B.C.
Andersen	1969	932/31-911/10	932/31-916/15
Begrich-Jepson	1929-1970	927/26-907	926-910
Miller	1967	925/23-905/03	925/23-908/07
Pavlovsky-Vogt	1964	931-910/09	931-914
Thiele (1895-1986)	1944, 1965, 1974	931/30-910/09	931/30-913

Israelite and Judaean History, Edited by John H. Hayes and J. Maxwell Miller, Philadelphia, Pennsylvania: The Westminster Press, 1977, 682, 683

A History of Israel in the New Testament Period, H. Jagersma, published 1979, translated by John Bowden from the Dutch 1982, First Fortress Press Edition 1983, Philadelphia, Pennsylvania: Fortress Press, Publisher, 268, 269

Appendix D

Dates given (B.C.) for the beginning of King Solomon's Temple:

    979 - Raven, (1910)
    969 - Kok, Kampen, Gispen,
    967 - E.R. Thiele (1951)
    966 - Leon J. Wood
         - J.B. Payne
         - E.R. Thiele (1965)
         - Merrill
         - Davis (1971, 1986)
    965   "   "   "
    962 - Begrich
    961 - Unger
    958 - Albright (1945)
         - Bright (1981)

   Several sources state that Solomon's Temple was begun in the Spring of Solomon's fourth year or 966 B.C. (I Kings 6:1) and it was completed seven years later in the fall (I Kings 6:38).

   "The year 966 is J.B. Payne's date for the commencement of the temple. Albright computes it at 958 (BASOR [Dec 1945]:17), E.R. Thiele at 967 (*Mysterious Numbers of the Hebrew Kings* [Grand Rapids: Eerdmans, 1951], p.254), and Begrich at 962. Unger personally prefers 961 (AOT, p.141), and thus puts the exodus at 1441. In the subsequent discussion, the writer uses the 966 date."

   A Survey of Old Testament Introduction, Gleason L. Archer, Jr., Chicago, Illinois: The Moody Bible Institute, Moody Press, 1974, 229

Appendix E

Over the centuries, numerous attempts have been made to assign dates to the events of the Old Testament. These dates in some cases have been several hundred years apart. For example, the date of Abraham's birth ranges from 1750 B.C. to 2166 B.C. according to varied chronologists. Likewise, the date given for the Exodus from Egypt has varied over the centuries. In the chart below, the approximate date of the proposal is followed by the date given for the Exodus.

Rabbi Jose	Ussher	Anstey	Unger	Anderson	Schult	Mauro
c.150	1650	1913	1954	1957	1960	1961
1311	1491	1612	1441	1290	1447	1533

Kitchen	Pfeiffer	Payne	Archer	Bright	Merrill	
1966	1973	1973	1974	1981	1987	
c.1280	1290	1446	1445	c.1280	1446	

Baker Encyclopedia of the Bible, Walter A. Elwell, General Editor, Grand Rapids, Michigan: Baker Book House, 1988, 450

Encyclopedia of Biblical Prophecy, J. Barton Payne, Grand Rapids, Michigan: Baker Book House, 1973, page xix

A Survey of Old Testament Introduction, Gleason L. Archer, Jr., Chicago, Illinois: Moody Bible Institute, Moody Press, 1974, 230

Appendix F

ADDITIONAL SUPPORT FOR THE EARLY DATE OF THE EXODUS

Professor Leon J. Wood (1918-1977), who pursued graduate studies in Israel through New York University and the Oriental Institute in Chicago, received the Ph.D. degree from Michigan State University and was Professor of Old Testament Studies and Dean of Grand Rapids Baptist Seminary stated:

> "The date of the Exodus, while debated even among conservative scholars, probably occurred shortly after the middle of the fifteenth century. This date, commonly placed c. 1446 B.C., is called the "early" date in contrast to one in the thirteenth century called the "late" date. Extensive evidence, both biblical and extrabiblical, bears on this determination. Suffice it now simply to list four biblical items that favor the early date. First, according to I Kings 6:1, the Exodus preceded the time when Solomon began to build the temple (c. 966 B.C.) by 480 years. Second, Jephthah says that by his day Israel had been in possession of the land for three hundred years (Judg. 11:26). Third, an analysis of the duration of the Judges' period seems to require more years than possible with the late date. Fourth, in looking at the sequence of events in Egyptian history, it may be safely argued that the biblical account fits well the fifteenth century but not in the thirteenth."

John C. Whitcomb, Th.D., former professor of Theology and Old Testament at Grace Theological Seminary, states: "If we follow Edwin R. Thiele's date of 931 B.C. for the end of Solomon's 40-year reign (*The Mysterious Numbers of the Hebrew Kings*, 2d ed.; Grand Rapids: Eerdmans, 1965), the Exodus must have occurred in 1445 B.C. by inclusive reckoning."

Timeline 2000

Archaeologists such as Joseph P. Free (1910-1974), Chairman of the Department of Archaeology at Wheaton College in Wheaton, Illinois, and later, Professor of Archaeology and History at Bemidji State College in Minnesota and Howard F. Vos, Professor of History and Archaeology at the King's College in Briarcliff Manor, New York, accept the Bible's evidence for the Exodus (c. 1446 B.C.), 480 years before the foundation of Solomon's Temple (circa 966-967 B.C.)

"According to I Kings 6:1, the Exodus took place 480 years before the fourth year of Solomon's reign, or about 1446...Many who cut themselves loose from the chronological specifics of the Old Testament place the patriarchal period in a general way during the first half of the second millennium B.C. Among such there is no unanimity of opinion in regard to the chronology of the patriarchs."

A Survey of Israel's History, Leon J. Wood, Revised by David O'Brien, Grand Rapids, Michigan: Zondervan Publishing House, Academie Books, 1986, 20

Old Testament Patriarchs and Judges Study-Graph, John C. Whitcomb, Th.D., Whitcomb Ministries, P.O. Box 277, Winona Lake, IN 46590, 1993, Introduction

Archaeology and Bible History, Joseph P. Free, Howard F. Vos, Grand Rapids, Michigan: Zondervan Publishing House, 1992, 45, 86, 87

PUBLICATIONS THAT USE AN EARLY DATE FOR THE EXODUS

Some publications that use an "early" date for the Exodus are given below: These dates are derived from a literal interpretation of I Kings 6:1 where the time from Soloman's Temple to the Exodus is given as 480 years. In the chart below, the date of publication is followed by the date given for the Exodus.

Cycles of Time and Seasons	Encyclopedia of Biblical Prophecy	Zondervan Pictorial Encyclopedia	The Bible Almanac	A Survey of Old Testament
1928 A.D.	1973 A.D.	1977 A.D.	1980 A.D.	1985 A.D.
1447 B.C.	1446 B.C.	1446/1445	1446 B.C.	1445 B.C.

Baker Ency. of the Bible	International Standard Bible Encyclopedia	The NIV Study Bible	The Ryrie Study Bible	Wycliffe Bible Ency
1988 A.D.	1989 A.D.	1984 A.D.	1994 A.D.	1980 A.D.
1447 B.C.	1447 B.C.	1446 B.C.	1445 B.C.	1445 B.C.

The Revell Bible Dictionary	A Popular Survey of the Old Testament	The International Inductive Study Bible
1990 A.D.	1977 A.D.	1993 A.D.
1446 B.C.	1445 B.C.	1445 B.C.

The New Chronological Bible	The Topical Chain Study Bible
1980 A.D.	1983 A.D.
1446 B.C.	c 1450 B.C.

Bibliography

Arthur, Kay. *God's Blueprint for Bible Prophecy*, Eugene, Oregon: Harvest House Publishers, 1995

Barna, George. *The Future of the American Family*, Chicago, Illinois: Moody Press, 1993

Barton, David. *America: To Pray Or Not To Pray?*, Aledo, Texas: WallBuilder Press, 1991

Barton, David. *Education and the Founding Fathers*, Aledo, Texas: Wall Builder Press, 1993

Bauer, Gary L. *Our Hopes, Our Dreams: A Vision for America*, Colorado Springs, Colorado: Focus on the Family Publishing, 1996

Ben-Gurion, David. *Ben-Gurion Looks at the Bible*, translated by Jonathan Kolatch, Middle Village, New York: Jonathan David Publishers, 1972

Ben-Gurion, David. edited and translated from the Hebrew under the supervision of Mordekhai Nurock, Minister of Israel in Australia, *Rebirth and Destiny of Israel*, New York, New York: Philosophical Library, Polyglot Press, 1954

Bennett, William J. *The Moral Compass*, New York, New York: Simon & Schuster, 1995

Bentwich, Norman and Helen. *Mandate Memories, 1918-1948*, New York, New York: Schocken Books, 1965

Bickerman, E.J. *Chronology of the Ancient World*, Ithaca, New York: Cornell University Press, 1968

Blackstone, W.E. *Jesus Is Coming*, New York, Chicago, London, Edinburgh: Fleming H. Revell Company, 1898, 1908, 1932

Blackstone, William E. foreword by John F. Walvoord, *Jesus Is Coming*, Grand Rapids, Michigan: Kregel Publications, 1989

Blanchard, John. *Gathered Gold*, Welwyn, Hertfordshire, England, Evangelical Press, 1984

Blumberg, Arnold. *Zion Before Zionism*, Syracuse, New York: Syracuse University Press, 1985

Carroll, B.H. D.D., LL.D., *The Inspiration of the Bible*, compiled and edited by J.B. Cranfill, M.D., LL.D., introduction by George W. Truett, D.D., and L.R. Scarborough, D.D., Christ For the World Publishers, Fleming H. Revell Company, 1930

Carter, Joseph. *1918: Year of Crisis, Year of Change*, Prentice-Hall, Printed in the United States, 1968

Carter, Tom. Compiler, *2200 Quotations from the Writings of Charles H. Spurgeon*, Grand Rapids, Michigan: Baker Books, 1988

Dobson, James C. Ph.D., *Family News From Dr. James Dobson*, Focus on the Family, July 1997

Doran, George H. *Great Britain, Palestine and the Jews*, New York: George H. Doran Company, 1918

Edwards, Tryon D.D., revised and enlarged by C.N. Catrevas, A.B. and Jonathan Edwards, A.M., *Useful Quotations*, New York, New York: Grosset & Dunlap, Publishers, Orsamus Turner Harris, 1933

Epp, Theodore H. Founder and Director, Back to the Bible Broadcast, *Practical Studies in Revelation, Volume II*, Lincoln, Nebraska: The Good News Broadcasting Association, 1969

Evans, Tony. *No More Excuses*, Wheaton, Illinois: Good News Publishers, Crossway Books, 1996

Finegan, Jack. *Handbook of Biblical Chronology, Principles of Time Reckoning in the Ancient World and Problems of Chronology in the Bible*, Princeton, New Jersey: Princeton University Press, 1964

Free, Joseph P. revised and expanded by Howard F. Vos, *Archaeology and Bible History*, Grand Rapids, Michigan: Zondervan Publishing House, 1992

Fromkin, David. *A Peace to End All Peace*, New York, New York: Avon Books, 1989

Graham, Billy. *Approaching Hoofbeats, The Four Horsemen of the Apocalypse*, Word Publishing, 1983

Grun, Bernard. *The Timetables of History*, New York, New York: Simon & Schuster, 1975

Hagee, John. *Beginning of the End*, Nashville, Tennessee: Thomas Nelson Publishers, 1996

Bibliography

Halff, Charles. *The End Times Are Here Now*, Co-published by 21st Century Press and Whitaker House, 1997

Halley, Henry H. *Halley's Bible Handbook*, Grand Rapids, Michigan: Zondervan Publishing House, 1965

Ironside, H. A. *The Four Hundred Silent Years* (From Malachi to Matthew), New York: Loizeaux Brothers, Bible Truth Press, 1914

James, William T., Editor, *Earth's Final Days*, Bob Anderson, Phil Arms, John Barela, Dave Breese, Steve Butler, J.R. Church, Don S. McAlvany, D.A. Miller, Chuck Missler, Lester Sumrall, David F. Webber, John Wesley White, William T. James, Green Forrest, Arkansas: New Leaf Press, 1994

James, William T., Editor, *Raging into Apocalypse*, Dave Breese, J.R. Church, Grant Jeffrey, David A. Lewis, Chuck Missler, Henry Morris, Gary Stearman, John Walvoord, David F. Webber, William T. James, Green Forest, Arkansas: New Leaf Press, 1995

James, William T. Editor, *The Triumphant Return of Christ*, Dave Breese, Ray Brubaker, John Barela, David A. Lewis, J.R. Church, Joseph J. Carr, Phil Arms, John Wesley White, William T. James, Green Forest, Arkansas: New Leaf Press, 1993

Jeremiah, David, with Carlson, C.C. *The Handwriting on the Wall*, Word Publishing, 1992; Tyler, Alexander. *Decline and Fall of the Athenian Republic*, 1748-1813

Johnston, Charles H.L. *Famous Generals of the Great War*, Boston, Massachusetts: The Colonial Press, C.H. Simonds Company, 1919

Kennedy, D. James with Black, Jim Nelson. *Character & Destiny, A Nation in Search of Its Soul*, Grand Rapids, Michigan: Zondervan publishing House, 1994

Kennedy, D. James. A.B., M.Div., D.D., D.Sac.Lit., Ph.D., Litt.D., D.Sac. Theol., D. Humane Let., *Why I Believe*, Word Publishing, 1980

Kohlenberger III, John R., Editor, *The One Minute Bible*, Bloomington, Minnesota: Garborg's Heart 'n Home, 1992

LaHaye, Tim and Beverly. *A Nation Without a Conscience*, Wheaton, Illinois: Tyndale House, 1994 (quote from Sproul taken from R. C. Sproul, "A Two-Handed King: Church and State Are Separate, but Also under God," *World*, 22 January 1994

LaHaye, Tim. *How to Study the Bible for Yourself*, Eugene, Oregon: Harvest House Publishers, 1976

Laurence, Richard. LL.D. translator *The Book of Enoch (I Enoch)*, (1821), reprinted by John Thompson, Glasgow (1882), Thousand Oaks, California: Artisan Sales, 1980

Lewis, Robert, with Campbell, Rich. *Real Family Values*, Gresham, Oregon: Vision House Publishing, 1995

Lutz, Ralph Haswell., translated by W.L. Campbell, *The Causes of the German Collapse in 1918*, Archon, 1969

Maddoux, Marlin. *America Betrayed!*, Shreveport, Louisiana: Huntington House, 1984

MacArthur, Jr., John. *The Christian and Government*, Chicago, Illinois: Moody Press, 1986

Mears, Henrietta C. *What the Bible is all About*, Minneapolis, Minnesota: Special Edition for The Billy Graham Evangelistic Association, Gospel Light Publications, 1966

McDowell, Josh. *Evidence that Demands a Verdict*, Thomas Nelson Publishers, Here's Life Publishers, Campus Crusade for Christ, 1979

McDowell, Josh and Stewart, Don. *Reasons Skeptics Should Consider Christianity*, A Campus Crusade for Christ Book, San Bernardino, California: Here's Life Publishers, 1981; (The Inspiration and Authority of the Bible)

McGee, J. Vernon. *J. Vernon McGee On Prophecy*, Nashville, Tennessee: Thomas Nelson Publishers, 1993

Morris, Henry M. Ph.D. *That You Might Believe*, A noted scientist shows that the Bible and true science are in harmony, Westchester, Illinois: Good News Publishers, 1978

Pentecost, J. Dwight. *Prophecy For Today*, Grand Rapids, Michigan: Zondervan Publishing House, 1961

Perkins, Bill., Editor, *Steeling the Mind of America*, Hal Lindsey, John Ankerberg, Henry Morris, Chuck Missler, Don McAlvany, Bill Perkins, Green Forest, Arkansas: New Leaf Press, 1995

Rogers, Adrian. *The Home on the Rock, Scriptural Principles for Building a Christian Home,* Love Worth Finding Ministries, P.O. Box

Bibliography

242000, Memphis, TN 38124, audio HOR-1

Rainey, Dennis. Adapted from *Lonely Husbands, Lonely Wives*, 1989 by Dennis Rainey. Published by Word, Dallas, Texas. Used by permission. Page 32 in *Growing a Healthy Marriage*, Copyright 1993 by Focus on the Family

Robertson, Pat. *The Turning Tide*, Dallas, London, Vancouver, Melbourne: Word Publishing, 1993, 271—James Madison, *Notes of Debates in the Federal Convention of 1787* (New York: Norton, 1987)

Ross, Hugh. Ph.D., *The Creator and the Cosmos*, Colorado Springs, Colorado: NavPress Publishing Group, 1993, 99, 100—William Paley, *Natural Theology and Attributes of Deity*, 18th ed. rev., Edinburgh, U.K.: Lackington, Allen and Co., and James Sawers, 1818

Ryrie, Charles C. *Ryrie's Concise Guide to the Bible*, San Bernardino, California: Here's Life Publishers, 1983

Savage, Raymond. preface by The Right Honourable David LLoyd George, P.C., M.P., *Allenby of Armageddon*, London, Great Britain: Hodder and Stoughton, 1925

Spurgeon, Charles H. *The Second Coming of Christ*, Chicago, Illinois: Fleming H. Revell Company, Moody Press, 1896

Stanley, Charles F. *The Great Escape*, Atlanta, Georgia: In Touch Ministries, P.O. Box 7900, 1989, Audio tape-PT279

Stewart, Don. *10 Reasons to Trust the Bible*, Orange, California: AusAmerica Publishers, 1990; (W. F. Albright, *The Christian Century*, November 1958) (Cited by H. H. Rowley, *Old Testament and Modern Study*) (Bernard Ramm, *Protestant Christian Evidences*, Chicago: Moody Press, 1957) (H. L. Hastings, as quoted by John Lea, *The Greatest Book in the World*. Philadelphia, PA: n.p., 1922)

Stowe, Harriet Beecher. *The Second Coming of Christ*, Harriet Beecher Stowe, D.W. Whittle, George Muller, Charles H. Spurgeon, J.C. Ryle, George C. Needham, Chicago, Illinois: Fleming H. Revell Company, Moody Press, 1896

Strauss, Lehman. *God's Plan For The Future*, Grand Rapids, Michigan: Zondervan Publishing House, 1965

Swindoll, Chuck. *The Strong Family*, Portland, Oregon: Multnomah Press, 1991

Thiele, Edwin R. *A Chronology of the Hebrew Kings*, Grand Rapids, Michigan: Academie Books, Zondervan, 1977

Thiele, Edwin R. *The Mysterious Numbers of the Hebrew Kings*, Grand Rapids, Michigan: The Zondervan Corporation, 1983, special edition by Kregel Publications, 1994

Thomas, Cal. *The Things that Matter Most*, New York, New York: HarperCollins Publishers, Zondervan, 1994

Varghese, Roy Abraham, Editor, *The Intellectuals Speak out About God*, 25 of the World's Greatest Living Philosophers and Scientists Reveal Why They Reject Atheism, Foreword by Ronald Reagan, Professor Charles Thaxton, Professor Robert Jastrow, Professor Chandra Wickramasinghe, Professor Henry Margenau, Sir John Eccles, Dr. Rupert Sheldrake, Professor Stanley L. Jaki, Professor Paul C. Vitz, Professor David Martin, Professor Stephen Schwarz, Professor Norman L. Geisler, Professor William Alston, Professor John E. Smith, Professor Alvin Plantinga, Professor Ralph McInerny, Bernard J.F. Lonergan, Professor William Craig, Professor Peter Kreeft, Professor Thomas Howard, Professor F.F. Bruce, Professor Wolfhart Pannenberg, Josh McDowell, Professor Nikolaus Lobkowicz, Sheldon Vanauken, Roy Abraham Varghese, *Evidence for Historical Accuracy of the New Testament*, Josh McDowell, Dallas, Texas: Lewis and Stanley Publishers, 1984

Wallbank, T. Walter and Taylor, Alastair M. and Bailkey, Nels M. *Civilization Past and Present*, Glenview, Illinois: Scott, Foresman and Company, 1975

Walvoord, John F. *Major Bible Prophecies, 37 Crucial Prophecies That Affect You Today*, Grand Rapids, Michigan: Zondervan Publishing House, 1991

Whitehouse, Arch. *Heroes and Legends of World War I*, Garden City, New York: Doubleday & Company, 1964

Wildman, Donald E. *The Home Invaders*, Wheaton, Illinois: Victor Books, a division of SP Publications, Inc., 1985

Bibliography

JEWISH HISTORY

Adams, J. McKee, Ph.D. Professor of Biblical Introduction in the Southern Baptist Theological Seminary Biblical Backgrounds, *A Geographical Survey of Bible Lands in the Light of the Scriptures and Recent Research*, Louisville, Kentucky, 1934, 106 (Exodus date: c. 1446 B.C.)

Akers, Rev. Peter, D.D., *Introduction to Biblical Chronology*, Cincinnatti, Ohio: Methodist Book Concern, R. P. Thompson, Printer, 1855, 331 (Exodus date: 1647-1646 B.C.)

Albright, William Foxwell. *The Biblical Period from Abraham to Ezra*, New York: Harper Torchbooks, Harper & Row Publishers, 1963, 12, 116, 117 (Exodus date: thirteenth century B.C.)

Anderson, Bernhard W. *Understanding the Old Testament*, fourth edition, Englewood Cliffs, New Jersey: Prentice-Hall, 1957, 1966, 1975, 1986, 646 (Exodus date: c. 1280 B.C.)

Anstey, Martin. Foreword by G. Cambell Morgan, *Chronology of the Old Testament*, Grand Rapids, Michigan: Kregel Publications, 1973, originally published as *The Romance of Bible Chronology* in two volumes by Marshall Brothers, London, 1913, Table 2, 160 (Exodus date: 1612 B.C.)

    The Long Chronology: Exodus dates
    Ussher 1491 B.C.
    A.V. Margin (Bishop Lloyd) 1491
    Bengel 1497
    Bede 1499
    Willis J. Beecher 1501
    Eusebius 1512
    Africanus 1525
    Petavius 1531
    The Short Chronology: Exodus dates
    Jewish Rabbinical Tradition 1314
    Owen C. Whitehouse 1320
    Barpm Bunsen 1328
    Lepsius 1328
    Third School: Exodus dates
    A.H. Sayce 1280
    E.A.W. Budge 1263

Breasted 1225
Flinders Petrie 1207

Arabs, Jews and the Promised Land, A Personal View of the Roots of the Conflict, Lakeland Florida, 1993

Archer, Jr., Gleason L. *A Survey of the Old Testament Introduction,* Chicago, Illinois: Moody Press, 1964, 1974, 1985, 230, 503 (Exodus date: 1445, 1446 B.C.)

Auchincloss, W. S., C.E., *Bible Chronology, From Abraham to the Christian Era,* New York, New York: D. Van Nostrand Company, 1905, 14 (Exodus date: 1477 B.C.)

Auchincloss, W.S. Auchincloss *Chronology of the Holy Bible,* introduction by A.H. Sayce, LL.D., Professor of Assyriology, Queen's College, Oxford, England, New York, New York: D. Van Nostrand Company, 1909, 46 (Exodus date: 1477 B.C.)

Barnavi, Eli., Gen. Editor. *A Historical Atlas of the Jewish People,* 1992, (Exodus date: 1290 B.C.)

Beecher, Willis Judson, D.D., *The Dated Events of the Old Testament,* New York and London: Harper & Brothers, The Sunday School Times Co., 1907, 71 (Exodus date: 1498 B.C.)

Ben-Gurion, David., Editor, *The Jews in their Land,* Garden City, New York: Doubleday & Company, 1974, 32 (Exodus date: c. 1286 B.C.E.)

Ben-Sasson, H.H., Editor, *A History of the Jewish People,* Cambridge, Massachusetts: Harvard University Press, English translation 1976 by George Weidenfeld and Nicolson, 42 (Exodus date: 13th century B.C.)

Bimson, John J. *Redating the Exodus and Conquest,* The Almond Press, P.O. Box 208 Sheffield, England, 1981, 232 (Exodus date: c. 1470 B.C.)

Birks, Rev. T.R., M.A., *The Exodus of Israel,* London, Great Britain: The Religious Tract Society, 1863 (Exodus date: none)

Boyd, Robert T. *Tells, Tombs and Treasure,* New York, New York: Bonanza Books, a division of Crown Publishers, by arrangement with Baker Book House, 1949, 108 (Exodus date: c. 1448 B.C.)

Breasted, James Henry. Late Director of the Oriental Institute in the

Bibliography

University of Chicago, *Ancient Times, A History of the Early World*, Boston: Ginn and Company, The Athenaeum Press, 1916, 1935, 220 (Exodus date: c. 13th & 14th century B.C.)

Bright, John. *A History of Israel*, third edition, Philadelphia, Pennsylvania: Westminster Press, 1959, 1972, 1981, 123, 124 Exodus date: 13th century B.C.)

Brown, Raymond D. S.S. *Recent Discoveries and the Biblical World*, Wilmington, Delaware: Michael Glazier, Inc., 1983, 70 (Exodus date: gives 1300-1280 B.C.)

Bruce, F.F. *Israel and the Nations*, Grand Rapids, Michigan: Wm. B. Eerdmans Publishing Company, 1963, 13 (Exodus date: c. 1300-1100 B.C.)

Burney, Rev. C.F. D. Litt., Oriel Professor of the Interpretation of Holy Scripture in the University of Oxford, Canon of Rochester, and fellow of St. John Baptist's College, Oxford, *The Book of Judges*, Prolegomenon by William F. Albright, New York, New York: KTAV Publishing House Inc., 1903, 1918, 1970, 6 (Exodus date: 13th century B.C., Albright prefers 1297 B.C.)

Buttrick, George Arthur. Commentary Editor, *The Interpreter's Bible*, Nashville, Tennessee: Abingdon Press, 1952, Vol. 1, 145 (Exodus date: 13th century B.C.)

Coffman, James Burton. *Commentary on Exodus*, Abilene, Texas: Abilene Christian University, A.C.U. Press, 1985, 6, 7 (Exodus date: c. 1440 B.C.)

Cole, R. Alan. PH.D., Master of Robert Menzies College, Macquarie University, *Exodus*, Downers Grove, Ill: 1973, 43 (Exodus date: c. 1260 B.C.)

Courville, Donovan A. *The Exodus Problem and its Ramifications*, Loma Linda, California: Challenge Books, 1971, 6-11 (Exodus date: 1445 B.C.)

Craghan, John F. *Exodus*, Collegeville, Minnesota: The Liturgical Press, 1985, 7 (Exodus date: C. 1250 B.C.)

Davies, G. Henton. *Exodus*, London, Great Britain: SCM Press, Northumberland Press, 1967, 38-41 (Exodus date: Both views)

Davis, John J. *Conquest and Crisis*, Grand Rapids, Michigan: Baker Book House, 1969, 18 (Exodus date: c. 1445 B.C.)

Davis, John J. *Moses and the Gods of Egypt, Studies in Exodus*, Grand Rapids, Michigan: Baker Book House and BMH Books, 1971, 1986, 34, 16-49 (Exodus date: 1446/1445 B.C., Very detailed, both views)

Dods, Rev. Marcus D.D., Whyte, Rev. Alexander, D.D., Macgregor, James, D.D., *Exodus, Handbooks for Bible Classes*, Edinburgh: T. & T. Clark, 1909 (Exodus date: c. 1500 B.C.)

Durham, John I. *Word Biblical Commentary*, Waco, Texas: Word Books, 1987, Exodus, Volume 3, (Exodus date: 13th century B.C.)

Dyer, Charles H. *The Date of the Exodus Reexamined, Bibliotheca Sacra*, July-Sept. 1983, Vol. 140, No.559, 234, 235 (Exodus date: 1445 B.C.)

Earle, Arthur. *The Bible Dates Itself*, 45 Tulip Circle, Southampton, Pennsylvania 18966, 1974, 196 (Exodus date: 1207 B.C.)

Ellison, H.L. *Exodus*, Edinburgh, Scoltland: Saint Andrew Press and Philadelphia, Pennsylvania: Westminister Press, 1982, (Exodus date: no date)

Faulstich, E.W. History, *Harmony & The Hebrew Kings*, Spencer, Iowa: Chronology Books, 1986, 196, 197 (Exodus date: 1461 B.C.)

Finegan, Jack. *Let My People Go*, New York and Evanston: Harper & Row, 1963, 18 (Exodus date: c. 1270 B.C.)

Finegan, Jack. *Light From the Ancient Past*, Princeton, New Jersey: Princeton University Press, London, England: Oxford University Press, 1946, 1959, 121 (Exodus date: 13th century B.C.)

Finegan, Jack. *Archaeological History of the Ancient Middle East*, Boulder, Colorado: Westview Press, 1979, 372, 420, 432 (Exodus date: Both views 13th Cent., 1447/1446 B.C.)

Free, Joseph P. and Vos, Howard F. *Archaeology and Bible History*, Grand Rapids, Michigan: Zondervan Publishing House, 1992, 45, 86, 87-89, 149-152. (Exodus date: c. 1440, 1446 B.C.)

Garstang, John. *Joshua and Judges*, London, England: Constable & Company, Oxford University Press, MacMillan Company, 1931, 54, 55, 56 (Exodus date: c. 1447 B.C.)

Garstang, John. *The Heritage of Solomon*, Great Britain: Harrison & Sons, Ltd., London, 1934, 137, 151 (Exodus date: c. 1440, 1447 B.C.)

Bibliography

Gaubert, Henri. *Moses and Joshua, Founders of the Nation*, New York, New York: Hastings House, 1969, 74 (Exodus date: c. 1220 B.C.)

Geisler, Norman L. *A Popular Survey of the Old Testament*, Grand Rapids, Michigan: Baker Book House, 1977, 54 (Exodus date: c. 1445 B.C.)

Gispen, W. H., translated by Ed van der Maas, Exodus, *Bible Student's Commentary*, Grand Rapids, Michigan: Zondervan Publishing House, 1982, 22, 23 (Exodus date: 1447 or c. 1445 B.C.)

Goodenow, Smith B. 1896, (Exodus date: 1591 B.C.)

Gordon, Cyrus H. *The Living Past*, New York, New York: Van Rees Press, 1941, 36, 37 (Exodus date: 13th century B.C.)

Govier, Gordon. New Evidence for Israeli Exodus, *Christianity Today*, Volume 39, No. 4, April 3, 1995, 87. (Exodus date: 15th century B.C.)

Gray, John. *Archaeology and the Old Testament World*, New York, New York: Harper Torchbooks, Harper & Row, 1965, 9, 92 (Exodus date: 13th century B.C.)

Grimmelsman, Rev. Henry J. *The Book of Exodus*, Norwood, Cincinnati, Ohio: Seminary Book Store, 1927, 232 (Exodus date: 1233-1223 B.C. ?)

Hall, H.R. M.A., D.Litt., F.S.A., Deputy-Keeper of Egyptian and Assyrian Antiquities, British Museum, *The Ancient History of the Near East*, London, England: Methuen & Co. LTD., 1913, 1920, 1924, 403, 404 (Exodus date: 13th century B.C.)

Hayes, John H. and Miller, J. Maxwell. *Israelite and Judaean History*, Philadelphia, Pennsylvania: Westminster Press, 1977, 151-154 (Exodus date: several views)

Hebert, Gabriel, D.D., *When Israel Came out of Egypt*, Guildford and London, Great Britain: SCM Press LTD, 1961, 62 (Exodus date: c. 1280, 1270 B.C.)

Herrmann, Siegfried. translated by James L. Blevins, *Time and History*, Nashville, Tennessee: Abingdon, Verlag W. Kohlhammer 1977, 1981, 37 (Exodus date: 1300-1200 B.C.)

Hill, Andrew E. and Walton, John H. *A Survey of the Old Testament*, Grand Rapids, Michigan: Zondervan Publishing House, A

Division of Harper Collins Publishers, 1991 (Exodus date: both views presented)

Huey, Jr., F.B. *Exodus*, Zondervan Publishing, 1977 (Exodus date: None)

Hyatt, J. Philip. *New Century Bible Commentary, Exodus*, Grand Rapids, Michigan: Wm. B. Eerdmans Publishing Company, 1971 by Marshall, Morgan & Scott, England, 43 (Exodus date: 13th century B.C.)

Jack, J.W., M.A., *The Date of the Exodus, In the Light of External Evidence*, Edinburgh: T&T Clark, London: Simpkin, Marshall, Hamilton, Kent, and Co. limited, New York: Charles Scribner's Books, 1925, 18, 19, 256, 257 (Exodus date: c. 1445 B.C.)

Jagersme, H. *A History of Israel in the Old Testament Period*, Philadelphia, Pennsylvania: Fortress Press, 1979, 47 (Exodus date: 13th century B.C.)

Johnstone, W. *Exodus*, Sheffield, England: Sheffield Academic Press, 1990, (Exodus date: 13th century B.C.)

Kelley, Page H. The King Who Did Not Know Joseph, *Illustrator*, Nashville, Tennessee: The Sunday School Board of the Southern Baptist Convention, Spring 1977, 49, 50 (Exodus date: 13th century B.C.)

Kenyon, Kathleen M. *Archaeology in the Holy Land*, New York, New York: Praeger Publishers, 1970, 206 (Exodus date: c. 1400-1200 B.C.)

Kenyon, Kathleen M. revised by P.R.S. Moorey, *The Bible and Recent Archaeology*, Atlanta, Georgia: John Knox Press, 1978, 1987 (Exodus date: None)

Kenyon, Sir Frederic. G.B.E. K.C.B. F.B.A. F.S.A., Sometime Director and Principal Librarian of the British Museum, *The Bible and Archaeology*, High Holborn, London: George G. Harrap & Co. Ltd., 1940, 74, 189 (Exodus date: c. 1420, c. 1440 B.C.)

Klassen, Frank R. *The Chronology of the Bible*, Nashville, Tennessee: Regal Publishers, 1975, 19, 20 (Exodus date: 1462 B.C.)

Kramer, Karl F. and Suelzer, Alexa. *A Chronological Chart of Salvation History*, New York, New York: Herder and Herder New York, 1968, 7 (Exodus date: c. 1280 B.C.)

Bibliography

Larsson, Gerhard. *The Secret System, A Study in the Chronology of the Old Testament*, 1973 by E.J. Brill, Leiden, Netherlands, 49 (Exodus date: c. 1440 B.C.)

Lepsius, Dr. Richard. *Letters from Egypt, Ethiopia, and the Peninsula of Sinai*, London, Great Britain: George Bell & Sons, 1853, 470-475

Lock, Walter, D.D., Editor, *The Book of Exodus*, Westminister Commentaries, Introduction and notes by A. H. McNeile, B.D., London, England: Methuen & Co., 1908, 13, 76

Luckenbill, D.D. *The American Journal of Theology*, Edited by the Divinity Faculty of the University of Chicago and Colleagues in Allied Departments, Volume XXII, January, 1918, Chicago, Illinois: The University of Chicago Press, *On Israel's Origins*, 37, 38, 40 (Exodus date: 1400-1300 B.C., Bohl 1414 B.C., Gressmann 1260-1225 B.C.)

MacGregor, Rev. James, D.D., *Exodus*, Edinburgh: T.&T. Clark, 1909 (Exodus date: c. 1500 B.C.)

Marston, Sir Charles, F.S.A. *New Bible Evidence, From the 1925-1933 Excavations*, New York, London and Edinburgh: Fleming H. Revell Company, 1934-35, 155-159 (Exodus date: 1447-1417 B.C.)

Mauro, Phillip. *The Chronology of the Bible*, New York, New York: George H. Doran Company, Hamilton Bros., 1922, 43 (Exodus date: 1533 B.C.)

McNeile, A.H., B.D., *The Book of Exodus*, Westminster Commentaries, London, Great Britain: Methuen and Co., London, 1908, 13, 76 (Exodus date: 1213, 1605, 1491 B.C.)

Merrill, Eugene H. *An Historical Survey of the Old Testament*, Grand Rapids, Michigan: Baker Book House, 1966, 98; 1991, 99 (Exodus date: 1446 B.C.)

Merrill, Eugene H., *Bibliotheca Sacra*, A Theological Quarterly Published by Dallas Theological Seminary, Fixed Dates in Patriarchal Chronology, , Vol. 137, July-September 1980, No. 547, 242, 248, 249 (Exodus date: 1446 B.C.)

Merrill, Eugene H. *Kingdom of Priests, A History of Old Testament Israel*, Grand Rapids, Michigan: Baker Book House, 1987 (Exodus date: 1446 B.C.)

Miller, Maxwell. *The Old Testament and the Historian*, Philadelphia,

Pennsylvania: Fortress Press, 1976, 78, 81 (Exodus date: 1300-1200 B.C.)

Millikin, Dr. Jimmy A. *Mid-America Theological Journal*, Studies in Exodus, Editor, Memphis, Tennessee: Mid-America Baptist Theological Seminary, Riverside Press, Fall 1977, Vol. 1, No. 1, 17 (Exodus date: 1447 B.C.)

Napier, B. Davie. *The Layman's Bible Commentary, The Book of Exodus*, Vol.3, Atlanta, Georgia: John Knox Press, 1963, 12-14 (Exodus date: 13th century B.C.)

Oesterley, W.O.E. and Robinson, Theodore H. *A History of Israel*, Great Britain: Oxford at the Clarendon Press, 1932, 71-73 (Exodus date: Refers to Jack's and Peet's works)

Olmert, Michael. CrossCurrents, When was the Exodus? The Volcano Knows, An Explosion over the Exodus, *Science*, June 86, 66 (Exodus date: 1477 B.C.-Hans Goedicke)

Panin, Ivan. Bible *Chronology in Three Parts*, 214 (Exodus date: 1466 B.C.)

Patten, Donald W. and Hatch, Ronald R. and Steinhauer, Loren C. *The Long Day of Joshua and Six other Catastrophies*, 199, 219 (Exodus date: 1447 B.C.)

Payne, J. Barton, Th.D. *An Outline of Hebrew History*, Grand Rapids, Michigan: Baker Book House, 1954 (Exodus date: 1446 B.C.)

Payne, J. Barton. *Encyclopedia of Biblical Prophecy*, Grand Rapids, Michigan: Baker Book House, 1973, page xix, (Exodus date: 1446 B.C.)

Peet, T. Eric. Brunner Professor of Egyptology in the University of Liverpool formerly Craven Fellow in the University of Oxford, *Egypt and the Old Testament*, Liverpool and London, England: The University Press of Liverpool LTD., Hodder and Stoughton LTD., 1923, 111, 112, 120 (Exodus date: Gives two schools: 1446 and 1220 B.C.)

Pfeiffer, Charles F. *Egypt and the Exodus*, Grand Rapids, Michigan: Baker Book House, 1964, 84-86 (Exodus date: Both views presented c. 1440, c. 1290 B.C.)

Pfeiffer, Charles F. *Old Testament History*, Grand Rapids, Michigan: Baker Book House, 1973, 28, 193 (Exodus date: Both views pre-

Bibliography

sented c. 1440, c. 1290 B.C.)

Phillips, John. *Bible Explorer's Guide*, Neptune, New Jersey: Loizeaux Brothers, 1987, 189 (Exodus Date: 1445 B.C.)

Ramsey, George W. *The Quest for the Historical Israel*, John Knox Press, 1981, 47-48 (Exodus date: 13th century B.C.)

Rendsburg, Gary A. *The Date of the Exodus and the Conquest/Settlement: The Case for the 1100s*, Vetus Testamentum, Vol. XLII, No. 4, Oct. 1992, 527. (Exodus date: 1175 B.C.) (Finkelstein's Date: 12th Cent., 510, Tel-Aviv, 1986) (Ussishkin's Date: 12th Cent., 514, London, 1985)

Robertson, Lieut. Colonel C.D., D.S.O., *On The Track of the Exodus*, 1990, 1 (Exodus date: 1447 B.C.)

Sarna, Nahum M. *Exploring Exodus*, New York, New York: Schocken Books, 1986, 8-13; 1996, 9, 10 (Exodus date: 13th century B.C.)

Savage, G.C., M.D., LL.D., F.A.C.S. *Cycles of Time and Seasons*, Nashville, Tennessee: Press of Marshall & Bruce Co., 1928 (Exodus date: 1447 B.C.)

Schatz, Elihu A. *Proof of the Accuracy of the Bible*, Middle Village, New York. Jonathan David Publishers, 1973, 47 (Exodus date: 1474 B.C.)

Schultz, Samuel J. *The Old Testament Speaks*, New York, New York: Harper & Row, 1980, 49 (Exodus date: c. 1450 B.C.)

Sloan, W.W. *A Survey of the Old Testament*, Nashville, Tennessee: Abingdon Press, 1957, 11 (Exodus date: c. 1250 B.C.)

Smith, William. L L.D., *Old Testament History, From Creation to the Return of the Jews from Captivity*, Author of *Smith's Bible Dictionary*, Joplin, Missouri: College Press, 1970, 163 (Exodus date: 1446 B.C.)

Soggin, J. Alberto. *A History of Ancient Israel*, Philadelphia, Pennsylvania: Westminster Press, 1984, 117 (Exodus date: prefers late date, 1300-1200 B.C.)

Stiebing, Jr., William H. *Out of the Dessert, Archaeology and the Exodus Conquest Narratives*, Buffalo, New York: Prometheus Books, 1988, 39-63 (Exodus date: 1300-1200 B.C.)

Thayer, Alexander Wheelock. *The Hebrews in Egypt and their Exodus*, Peoria, Illinois: Edw. Hine & Co., 1897 by E.S. Willcox (Exodus date: None)

Thiele, Edwin R. *A Chronology of the Hebrew Kings*, Grand Rapids, Michigan: Academie Books, Zondervan Publishing House (Exodus date: none)

Thompson, J.A., Lecturer in Old Testament Studies, Baptist Theological College, New South Wales, Australia, *The Bible and Archaeology*, Grand Rapids, Michigan: Wm. B. Eerdmans Publishing Co., 1962, 55, 63 (Exodus date: c. 1280, also gives c. 1440 B.C. view)

Toffteen, Olaf A., Ph.D., Professor of Semitic Languages and Old Testament Literature Western Theological Seminary, *The Historic Exodus*, Chicago, Illinois: University of Chicago Press, 1909, 234, 235, 270 (Exodus date: Both views given, 1447 & c. 1144 B.C.)

Unger, Merrill F. *Introductory Guide to the Old Testament*, Grand Rapids, Michigan: Zondervan Publishing House, 1951, 198 (Exodus date: c. 1442 B.C.)

Vos, Howard F. *Archaeology in Bible Lands*, Chicago, Illinois: Moody Bible Institute, Moody Press, 1977, 240, 241 (Exodus date: Both views given)

Waltke, Bruce K. *Palestinian Artifactual Evidence Supporting the Early Date of the Exodus, Bibliotheca Sacra*, January-March 1972, Vol. 129, No. 513, 33 (Exodus date: c. 1440 B.C.)

Walton, John H. *Chronological and Background Charts of the Old Testament*, Grand Rapids, Michigan: Zondervan Publishing House, 1994 (Exodus date: Both views given)

Whitcombe, John C. Th.D., *Old Testament Patriarchs and Judges Studygraph*, Winona Lake, Indiana: Whitcombe Ministries, 1993

Wilson, Ian. *The Exodus Enigma*, London, England: Weidenfeld and Nicolson, 1985, Introd., 18-20 (Exodus date: 1300-1200 B.C.)

Wilson, Ian. *Exodus, The True Story Behind the Biblical Account*, Harper & Row Publishers, San Francisco, London, Mexico City, Sao Paulo, Singapore, Sydney, l985, 19, 20 (Exodus date: 13th century B.C.)

Wood, Leon T. and Payne, J. Barton, Editor, *New Perspectives on the Old Testament, Date of the Exodus*, Waco, Texas and London, England: Word Books, 1970, 66-87 (Exodus date: 1446 B.C.)

Wood, Leon J. revised by David O'Brien, *A Survey of Israel's History*,

Grand Rapids, Michigan: Zondervan Corporation, 1970, 1986, 20, 69. (Exodus date: 1446 B.C.)

Youngblood, Ronald F. *Exodus*, Chicago, Illinois: Moody Press, 16 1983 (Exodus date: 1445 B.C.)

OTTOMAN HISTORY

Bacharach, Jere L. A *Near East Studies Handbook*, 570-1974, University of Washington Press, 1974

Bakhit, Muhammad Adnan. PH.D., *The Ottoman Province of Damascus in the 16th Century*, Beirut, Lebanon: Printed in Lebanon, Designed and photoset by Hassib Dergham & Sons, Beirut, Librairie du Liban, 1982

Holt, P. M. Professor of Arab History in the University of London, *Egypt and the Fertile Crescent: 1516-1922*, Ithaca, New York: Cornell University Press, Longmans Green and Co., London, l966

Howard, Harry N. *The Partition of Turkey: 1913-1923*, University of Oklahoma Press, 1931

Inalcik, Halil. translated by Norman Itzkowitz and Colin Imber, *The Ottoman Empire, The Classical Age: 1300-1600*, London, Great Britain: Weidenfeld and Nicolson: Praeger Publishers, Inc., 1973

Kinross, Lord. *The Ottoman Centuries, The Rise and Fall of the Turkish Empire*, New York, New York: William Morrow and Company, 1977

Palmer, Alan. *The Decline & Fall of the Ottoman Empire*, New York: Barnes & Noble by arrangement with Campbell Thompson & McLaughlin, 1992

Peters, F.E. Jerusalem, *The Holy City in the Eyes of Chroniclers, Visitors, Pilgrims, and Prophets from the Days of Abraham to the Beginnings of Modern Times*, Princeton, New Jersey: Princeton University Press, 1985

Pitcher, Donald Edgar. *An Historical Geography of the Ottoman Empire*, From Earliest Times to the End of the Sixteenth Century, The Shield Press, 1968, 1972

Pitcher, Donald Edgar. *An Historical Geography of the Roman Empire*, Great Britain: Shield Press, 1972; Leiden, Netherlands: E.J. Brill, 1968

Shaw, Stanford J. *History of the Ottoman Empire and Modern Turkey*, Vol. l- *Empire of the Gazis: The Rise and Decline of the Ottoman Empire*, 1280-1808, Cambridge Univ Press, 1976

Stripling, George William Frederick. *The Ottoman Turks and the Arabs, 1511-1574*, Urbana, Illinois: University of Illinois Press, Illinois Studies in the Social Sciences, Vol. 26, No. 4, 1942

Zeine, Z.N. *Arab-Turkish Relations and the Emergence of Arab Nationalism*, 1958

PERIODICALS AND REFERENCE BOOKS

Christianity Today, A New Look at an Old Problem: The Date of the Exodus, Vol. 26, No.20, Dec. 17, 1982, 58-60 (Exodus date: Reviews Early and Late Dates)

Christianity Today, April 3, 1995, quoted in *Bible in the News*, July 1995, Southwest Radio Church, P.O. Box 1144, Oklahoma City, Oklahoma, New Evidence for the Israeli Exodus, 18 (Exodus date: Update on views)

Encyclopedia Britannica, 1989

Encyclopedia of Zionism and Israel, Editor: Raphael Patai, New York, New York: Herzl Press/McGraw-Hill, 1971

Great Britain, Palestine and the Jews, New York, New York: George H. Doran Company, 1918

1996 Information Please Almanac, Otto Johnson, Editor, New York, New York: Houghton Mifflin Company, 1995

Jewish History Atlas, Martin Gilbert, Macmillan Company, 1969

Studies in Exodus, Mid-America Theological Journal, (Exodus date: 1447)

The Bible Almanac, James I. Packer, Merrill C. Tenney, William White, Jr., Nashville, Tennessee: Thomas Nelson Publishers, 1980

The Cambridge Ancient History, Vol. III, Part 1, The Prehistory of the Balkans; and the Middle East and the Aegean World, Tenth to Eighth Centuries B.C., Editors: John Boardman, I.E.S. Edwards, N. G. L. Hammond, E. Sollberger, Cambridge University Press, 1982

The Columbia History of the World, Edited by John A. Garraty and Peter Gay, Harper & Row, Publishers, 1972

Bibliography

The Companion Bible, Grand Rapids, Michigan: Kregel Publications, 1990

The Expositors Bible Commentary, Grand Rapids, Michigan: Zondervan Publishing House, 1979, 261 (Exodus date: Both views; leans towards 13th century B.C. date)

The International Standard Bible Encyclopedia, Geoffrey W. Bromiley, Everett F. Harrison, Roland K. Harrison, William Sanford LaSor, Edgar W. Smith, Jr. Editors, Grand Rapids, Michigan: William B. Eerdmans Publishing Company, 1979

The New Unger's Bible Dictionary, Merrill F. Unger, Chicago, Illinois: Moody Press, 1988

The Revell Bible Dictionary, General Editor: Lawrence O. Richards, Ph.D., Old Tappan, New Jersey: Fleming H. Revell Company, 1990

The Zondervan Pictorial Encyclopedia of the Bible, Merrill C. Tenney, Ph.D., General Editor, Grand Rapids, Michigan: The Zondervan Corporation, 1976

Vetus Testamentum, Vol. XLII, No. 4, October 1992, E. J. Brill, Leiden, the Netherlands, 527 (Exodus date: 1175 B.C.)

Webster's Seventh New Collegiate Dictionary, Springfield, Massachusetts: G & C Merriam Company, 1963

Notes

Chapter One

1. *Halley's Bible Handbook*, Henry H. Halley, Grand Rapids, Michigan: Zondervan Publishing House, 1965, 18
2. *Ben-Gurion Looks at the Bible*, translated by Jonathan Kolatch, Middle Village, New York: Jonathan David Publishers, 1972, 294
3. *Halley's Bible Handbook*, 18
4. *Ryrie's Concise Guide to the Bible*, Charles C. Ryrie, San Bernardino, California: Here's Life Publishers, 1983, 12
5. *What the Bible is all About*, Henrietta C. Mears, Minneapolis, Minnesota: Special Edition for The Billy Graham Evangelistic Association, Gospel Light Publications, 1966, 1, 6
6. *Evidence that Demands a Verdict*, Josh McDowell, Thomas Nelson Publishers, Here's Life Publishers, Campus Crusade for Christ, 1979, 16
7. *God's Plan For the Future*, Lehman Strauss, Grand Rapids, Michigan: Zondervan Publishing House, 1965, 7
8. *The One Minute Bible*, John R. Kohlenberger III, Editor, Bloomington, Minnesota: Garborg's Heart 'n Home, Inc., 1992, 265
9. *Webster's Seventh New Collegiate Dictionary*, Springfield, Massachusetts: G & C Merriam Company, 1963, 438
10. *2200 Quotations from the Writings of Charles H. Spurgeon*, Tom Carter, Compiler, Grand Rapids, Michigan: Baker Books, 1988, 24
11. *Reasons Skeptics Should Consider Christianity*, Josh McDowell and Don Stewart, A Campus Crusade for Christ Book, San Bernardino, California: Here's Life Publishers, 1981, 21; (The Inspiration and Authority of the Bible, 173)
12. *The Inspiration of the Bible*, B.H. Carroll, D.D., LL.D., compiled and edited by J.B. Cranfill, M.D., LL.D., Introduction by George W. Truett, D.D., and L.R. Scarborough, D.D., Christ For the World Publishers, Inc., Fleming H. Revell Company, 1930, 122
13. *10 Reasons to Trust the Bible*, Don Stewart, Orange, California:

Timeline 2000

AusAmerica Publishers, 1990, 24; (W. F. Albright, *The Christian Century,* November 1958)
14. *Halley's Bible Handbook*, 19
15. Ibid., 18
16. *That You Might Believe, A Noted Scientist Shows That The Bible and True Science are in Harmony,* Henry M. Morris, Ph.D., Westchester, Illinois: Good News Publishers, 1978, 39
17. *Halley's Bible Handbook*, 19
18. *Why I Believe,* D. James Kennedy, A.B., M.Div., D.D., D.Sac.Lit., Ph.D., Litt.D., D.Sac. Theol., D. Humane Let., Word Publishing, 1980, 36
19. *10 Reasons to Trust the Bible,* 33; (Cited by H. H. Rowley, Old Testament and Modern Study, 25)
20. *That You Might Believe,* 109
21. *The Intellectuals Speak Out About God, 25 of the World's Greatest Living Philosophers and Scientists Reveal Why They Reject Atheism,* Foreword by Ronald Reagan, Edited by Roy Abraham Varghese, Professor Charles Thaxton, Professor Robert Jastrow, Professor Chandra Wickramasinghe, Professor Henry Margenau, Sir John Eccles, Dr. Rupert Sheldrake, Professor Stanley L. Jaki, Professor Paul C. Vitz, Professor David Martin, Professor Stephen Schwarz, Professor Norman L. Geisler, Professor William Alston, Professor John E. Smith, Professor Alvin Plantinga, Professor Ralph McInerny, Bernard J.F. Lonergan, Professor William Craig, Professor Peter Kreeft, Professor Thomas Howard, Professor F.F. Bruce, Professor Wolfhart Pannenberg, Josh McDowell, Professor Nikolaus Lobkowicz, Sheldon Vanauken, Roy Abraham Varghese, *Evidence for Historical Accuracy of the New Testament,* Josh McDowell, Dallas, Texas: Lewis and Stanley Publishers, 1984, 293-294.
22. *10 Reasons to Trust the Bible,* 46; (Bernard Ramm, Protestant Christian Evidences, Chicago: Moody Press, 1957, 232-233)
23. *Gathered Gold,* John Blanchard, Welwyn, Hertfordshire, England: Evangelical Press, 1984, 18
24. *10 Reasons to Trust the Bible,* 46, 47; (H. L. Hastings, as quoted by John Lea, *The Greatest Book in the World.* Philadelphia, PA: n.p., 1922,pp. 17,18)

Chapter Two

1. *Gathered Gold*, 19
2. *Ben-Gurion Looks at the Bible*, 46

Footnotes

3. *Gathered Gold*, 23
4. *How to Study the Bible for Yourself*, Tim LaHaye, Eugene, Oregon: Harvest House Publishers, 1976, 25
5. *Gathered Gold*, 19
6. Ibid., 19
7. Ibid., 22
8. Ibid., 19
9. *Beginning of the End*, John Hagee, Nashville, Tennessee: Thomas Nelson Publishers, 1996, 45
10. *Raging into Apocalypse*, Dave Breese, J.R. Church, Grant Jeffrey, David A. Lewis, Chuck Missler, Henry Morris, Gary Stearman, John Walvoord, David F. Webber, William T. James, Green Forest, Arkansas: New Leaf Press, 1995, 261
11. *Prophecy For Today*, J. Dwight Pentecost, Grand Rapids, Michigan: Zondervan Publishing House, 1961, 13
12. *The Second Coming of Christ*, Harriet Beecher Stowe, D.W. Whittle, George Muller, Charles H. Spurgeon, J.C. Ryle, George C. Needham, Chicago, Illinois: Fleming H. Revell Company, Moody Press, 1896, 17
13. *Jesus Is Coming*, W.E.B., New York; Chicago; London; Edinburgh: Fleming H. Revell Company, 1898, 1908, 1932, 177
14. *God's Blueprint for Bible Prophecy*, Kay Arthur, Eugene, Oregon: Harvest House Publishers, 1995, 28

Chapter Three

1. *The Creator and the Cosmos*, Hugh Ross, Ph.D., Colorado Springs, Colorado: NavPress Publishing Group, 1993, 99, 100—William Paley, *Natural Theology and Attributes of Deity*, 18th ed. rev., Edinburgh, U.K.: Lackington, Allen and Co., and James Sawers, 1818, 12-14
2. Ibid., 100
3. *The Bible Almanac*, James I. Packer, Merrill C. Tenney, William White, Jr., Nashville, Tennessee: Thomas Nelson Publishers, 1980, 44
4. The 1964 system of Astronomical constants was replaced in 1984 so that the tropical year of reference (1900) contained 31 556 925.974 7 ephemeris seconds. The length of the ordinary, tropical, or solar year, as it is called, on which we base our calendars, was 365.242 190 days or 365 days, 5 hours, 48 minutes, 45.3 seconds for the year

1991. *The Astronomical Almanac* for the year 1991 (Data for Astronomy, Space Sciences, Geodesy, Surveying, Navigation and other applications) Issued by the Nautical Almanac Office, United States Naval Observatory by direction of the Secretary of the Navy and under the authority of Congress, Washington: U.S. Government Printing Office, 1990, K5, C1

5. *The Book of Enoch* (*I Enoch*), Richard Laurence, LL.D. Translator (1821), Reprinted by John Thompson, Glasgow (1882), Thousand Oaks, California: Artisan Sales, 1980, 7,8

6. The rotation of the earth around the sun is decreasing at the rate of 0.530 seconds per century (0.0053 seconds per year). The 1991 *World Almanac and Book of Facts*, page 276. Consequently, an eclipse of the sun or moon calculated for the year 500 B.C. (around 2500 years ago) could be predicted to occur within 15 seconds of its onset (0.53 times 25 centuries = 13.25 seconds error). Including the coefficient of change (0.530 seconds per century) in the calculations reduces the error to near zero.

7. *The Mysterious Numbers of the Hebrew Kings*, Edwin R. Thiele, Grand Rapids, Michigan: The Zondervan Corporation, 1983, special edition by Kregel Publications, 1994, 229

8. *The Zondervan Pictorial Encyclopedia of the Bible*, Merrill C. Tenney, Ph.D., General Editor, Grand Rapids, Michigan: The Zondervan Corporation, 1976, Vol. 1, 830

9. *The Bible Almanac*, 44, 45

10. *The International Standard Bible Encyclopedia*, Geoffrey W. Bromiley, Everett F. Harrison, Roland K. Harrison, William Sanford LaSor, Edgar W. Smith, Jr., Editors, Grand Rapids, Michigan: William B. Eerdmans Publishing Company, 1979, 686

11. *Archaeology and Bible History*, Joseph P. Free, revised and expanded by Howard F. Vos, Grand Rapids, Michigan: Zondervan Publishing House, 1992, 242

12. *A Chronology of the Hebrew Kings*, Edwin R., Thiele, Grand Rapids, Michigan: Academie Books, Zondervan, 1977, 7

Chapter Four

1. *The Mysterious Numbers of the Hebrew Kings*, 33, 15
2. Ibid., 33
3. Ibid., 15, 16
4. *Archaeology and Bible History*, 151

Footnotes

5. *The Mysterious Numbers of the Hebrew Kings*, 23, 24
6. *Kingdom of Priests*, A History of Old Testament Israel, Eugene H. Merrill, Grand Rapids, Michigan: Baker Book House, 1987, 67
7. (A review of the 1951 copyrighted version by Gleason L. Archer)
8. *Archaeology and Bible History*, 151
9. *Israelite and Judaean History*, Edited by John H. Hayes and J. Maxwel Miller, Philadelphia, Pennsylvania: The Westminster Press, 1977, 682, 683
10. *Archaeology and Bible History*, 151, 152—See also: appendix B and C
11. Ibid., 151, 152
12. Some calculate the fourth year at 965 B.C.
13. See appendix B, C, D
14. *Kingdom of Priests*, 31—See also: *An Outline of Hebrew History*, J. Barton Payne, Th.D., Grand Rapids, Michigan: Baker Book House, 1954, 34, 35

Chapter Five

1. *The Date of the Exodus, In the Light of External Evidence,* J.W. Jack, M.A., Edinburgh, Great Britain: Printed by Morrison and Gibb for T & T Clark, 1925, Preface v, vi, 199
2. *Archaeology and Bible History*, Joseph P. Free, Howard F. Vos, Grand Rapids, Michigan: Zondervan Publishing House, 1992, 45
3. See appendix E and the following references:

   The Book of Exodus, Westminister Commentaries, Edited by Walter Lock D.D., Introduction and notes by A. H. Mcneile, B.D., London, England: Methuen & Co., 1908, 13, 76;

   Introduction to Biblical Chronology, Rev. Peter Akers, D.D., Cincinnati, Ohio: Methodist Book Concern, R. P. Thompson, Printer, 1855, 211, 227, 229, 231, 240, 241, 331;

   Letters from Egypt, Ethiopia, and the Peninsula of Sinai, Dr. Richard Lepsius, London, Great Britain: George Bell & Sons, 1853, 470-475
4. *When Israel Came out of Egypt*, Gabriel Hebert, D.D., Guildford and London, Great Britain: SCM Press LTD, 1961, 44. Also see Hastings, Dictionary of the Bible (1898), art. 'Chronology of the Bible', Vol. I, pp. 398-9; S.R. Driver's commentry on Exodus (CUP, 1911); Flinders Petrie, Egypt and Israel (SPCK, 1911).
5. Ibid., 44

(Thotmes III- i.e.Thutmose III (Thutmosis Thothmes) dates later adjusted to 1482-1447)

A Survey of Old Testament Introduction, Gleason L. Archer, Jr., Chicago, Illinois: Moody Bible Institute, Moody Press, 1974, 503

6. Ibid., 230

   Kingdom of Priests, 111

   When Israel Came out of Egypt, 44

   Also see J.W.Jack, *The Date of the Exodus*, T. and T. Clark, 1925

   Joshua—Judges, John Garstang, Glasgow, Great Britain: Printed by Robert Maclehose and Co. for Constable & Company Ltd, 1931, 54, 55, W. J. Phythian-Adams, *The Call of Israel*, 1934

7. *Archaeology and Bible History*, 79, 80, 87—See Bryant G. Wood, "Did the Israelites Conquer Jericho?" *Biblical Archaeology Review* (March/April 1990), 57.

8. *The Date of the Exodus*, 18, 19

9. Ibid., 257

10. Ibid., 201

11. *When Israel Came out of Egypt*, 44, 45

12. *A Survey of Old Testament Introduction*, 231

    A Survey of The Old Testament, Andrew C. Hill & John H. Walton, Grand Rapids, Michigan: Zondervan Publishing House, A Division of Harper Collins Publishers, 1991, 107-109

13. *Chronological and Background Charts of the Old Testament*, John H. Walton, Grand Rapids, Michigan: Zondervan Publishing House, 1994, 99, 102, 103

    A Survey of the Old Testament, 107-109

14. *The Bible Almanac*, Editors J.I. Packer, Merrill C. Tenney, William White, Jr., Nashville, Tennessee: Thomas Nelson Publishers, 1980, 50, 51

15. *The Bible Almanac*, 51

16. *The Zondervan Pictorial Encyclopedia of the Bible*, Volume one, 833, 834

17. *Kingdom of Priests*, 67

18. *A Survey of Old Testament Introduction*, 230, 231, 503

19. *The New Unger's Bible Dictionary*, Merrill F. Unger, Chicago, Illinois: Moody Press, 1988, 385

20. *Kingdom of Priests*, 68, 69, 75

21. *Encyclopedia of Biblical Prophecy*, J. Barton Payne, Grand Rapids, Michigan: Baker Book House, 1973, page xix

22. Other Old Testament professors and publications that have adopted

the "early date" view of the Exodus are listed in appendix F.
23. *The Zondervan Pictorial Encyclopedia of the Bible*, 835
24. *Old Testament Patriarchs and Judges Studygraph*, John C. Whitcomb, Th.D., Winona Lake, Indiana: Whitcomb Ministries, 1993
25. *The International Standard Bible Encyclopedia*, General Editor Geofrey W. Bromiley, Grand Rapids, Michigan: William B. Eerdmans Publishing Company, c. 1979, 680
26. *A Survey of Israel's History*, Leon J. Wood, Revised by David O'Brien, Grand Rapids, Michigan: Zondervan Corporation, 1986, 84, 391
27. *Kingdom of Priests*, 225

Chapter Six

1. *Useful Quotations*, Tryon Edwards, D.D., Revised and enlarged by C.N. Catrevas, A.B. and Jonathan Edwards, A.M., New York, New York: Grosset & Dunlap, Publishers, Orsamus Turner Harris, 1933, 451
2. Ibid., 255
3. Ibid., 255
4. *Kingdom of Priests*, 505.
5. *The Companion Bible*, Grand Rapids, Michigan: Kregel Publications, 1990, Appendix, 69
6. *Archaeology and Bible History*, 242
7. *Civilization Past and Present*, T. Walter Wallbank, Alastair M. Taylor, Nels M. Bailkey, Glenview, Illinois: Scott, Foresman and Company, 1975, 135
8. *Allenby of Armageddon*, Raymond Savage with a preface by The Right Honourable David LLoyd George, P.C., M.P., London, Great Britain: Hodder and Stoughton, 1925, 197
9. Ibid., 283
10. *Great Britain, Palestine and the Jews*, George H. Doran Company, New York, 1918, Preface v
11. *Mandate Memories*, 1918-1948, Norman and Helen Bentwich, New York, New York: Schocken Books, 1965, 9

(Norman Bentwich, a legal officer in the Military Administration of Palestine, 1918-20, and in the Government of the Mandatory Power, 1920-31 and a part-time Chair of International Relations at the Hebrew University of Jerusalem, during the remaining period of the Mandate and the first three years of Israel.)

Timeline 2000

12. *Allenby of Armageddon*, 15
13. *The Columbia History of the World*, Edited by John A. Garraty and Peter Gay, Harper & Row, Publishers, 1972, 423
14. *A Peace to End All Peace*, David Fromkin, New York, New York: Avon Books, 1989, 291

Chapter Seven

1. *The Ottoman Turks and the Arabs*, 1511-1574, George William Frederick Stripling, Urbana, Illinois: The University of Illinois Press, Illinois Studies in the Social Sciences, Vol XXVI, No. 4, 1942, 58
2. *The Ottoman Province of Damascus in the 16th Century*, Muhammad Adnan Bakhit, PH.D., Beirut, Lebanon: Printed in Lebanon, Designed and photoset by Hassib Dergham & Sons, Beirut, Librairie du Liban, 1982, 19
3. *Egypt and the Fertile Crescent*, 1516-1922, P.M. Holt, Professor of Arab History in the University of London, Ithaca, New York: Cornell University Press, no date, 43
4. *An Historical Geography of the Roman Empire*, Donald Edgar Pitcher, Great Britain: Shield Press, 1972; Leiden, Netherlands: E.J. Brill, 1968, 105
5. *Egypt and the Fertile Crescent*, 277
6. *Arabs, Jews and the Promised Land*, A Personal View of the Roots of the Conflict, Lakeland Florida, 1993, 1
7. *Major Bible Prophecies, 37 Crucial Prophecies That Affect You Today*, John F. Walvoord, Grand Rapids, Michigan: Zondervan Publishing House, 1991, 85

Chapter Eight

1. *J. Vernon McGee On Prophecy*, J. Vernon McGee, Nashville, Tennessee: Thomas Nelson Publishers, 1993, 57
2. *God's Blueprint for Bible Prophecy*, 81, 82
3. *The End Times Are Here Now*, Charles Halff, Co-published by 21st Century Press and Whitaker House, 1997, 73, 36
4. *J. Vernon McGee On Prophecy*, 55
5. *The Triumphant Return of Christ*, Dave Breese, Ray Brubaker, John Barela, David A. Lewis, J.R. Church, Joseph J. Carr, Phil Arms, John Wesley White, William T. James, Green Forest, Arkansas: New Leaf Press, 1993, 312

Footnotes

6. *J. Vernon McGee On Prophecy*, 54
7. *A Peace to End All Peace*, David Fromkin, New York, New York: Avon Books, 1989, 15
8. *1918: Year of Crisis, Year of Change*, Joseph Carter, Printed in the United States of America, Prentice Hall, 1968, Introduction vii, viii, ix

Chapter Nine

1. *Approaching Hoofbeats, The Four Horsemen of the Apocalypse,* Billy Graham, Word Publishing, 1983, 209
2. *America Betrayed!*, Marlin Maddoux, Shreveport, Louisiana: Huntington House Inc., 1984, 45
3. *Steeling the Mind of America*, Hal Lindsey, John Ankerberg, Henry Morris, Chuck Missler, Don McAlvany, Bill Perkins, Green Forest, Arkansas: New Leaf Press, 1995, 103.
4. *1996 Information Please Almanac*, Otto Johnson, Editor, New York, New York: Houghton Mifflin Company, 1995, 360
5. *Jesus Is Coming*, William E. Blackstone, foreword by John F. Walvoord, Grand Rapids, Michigan: Kregel Publications, 1989, 64
6. *The Second Coming of Christ*, Charles H. Spurgeon, Chicago, Illinois: Fleming H. Revell Company, Moody Press, 1896, 117, 118

Chapter Ten

1. *Character & Destiny, A Nation in Search of Its Soul*, D. James Kennedy with Jim Nelson Black, Grand Rapids, Michigan: Zondervan Publishing House, 1994, 11
2. *The Christian and Government*, John MacArthur, Jr., Chicago, Illinois: Moody Press, 1986, 34
3. *America: To Pray Or Not To Pray?*, David Barton, Aledo, Texas: WallBuilder Press, 1991
4. *J. Vernon McGee On Prophecy*, 36
5. *Practical Studies in Revelation*, Volume II, Theodore H. Epp, Founder and Director, Back to the Bible Broadcast, Lincoln, Nebraska: The Good News Broadcasting Association, Inc., 1969, 11
6. *Earth's Final Days*, Bob Anderson, Phil Arms, John Barela, Dave Breese, Steve Butler, J.R. Church, Don S. McAlvany, D.A. Miller, Chuck Missler, Lester Sumrall, David F. Webber, John Wesley White, William T. James, Green Forest, Arkansas: New Leaf Press, 1994, 259, 260, 272

7. *Education and the Founding Fathers*, David Barton, Aledo, Texas: Wallbuilder Press, 1993, 19, 20
8. *Halley's Bible Handbook*, 18
9. *The Home on the Rock, Scriptural Principles for Building a Christian Home*, Adrian Rogers, Love Worth Finding Ministries, P.O. Box 242000, Memphis, TN 38124, audio HOR-1
10. *Real Family Values*, Robert Lewis with Rich Campbell, Gresham, Oregon: Vision House Publishing, 1995, 11
11. *The Moral Compass*, William J. Bennett, New York, New York: Simon & Schuster, 1995, 15
12. *Our Hopes, Our Dreams: A Vision for America*, Gary L. Bauer, Colorado Springs, Colorado: Focus on the Family Publishing, 1996, 47
13. *Halley's Bible Handbook*, 19
14. *The Strong Family*, Chuck Swindoll, Portland, Oregon: Multnomah Press, 1991, 24
15. *Halley's Bible Handbook*, 18
16. *Adapted from Lonely Husbands, Lonely Wives*, 1989 by Dennis Rainey. Published by Word, Inc., Dallas, Texas; page 32 in Growing a Healthy Marriage, 1993 by Focus on the Family
17. *The Future of the American Family*, George Barna, Chicago, Illinois: Moody Press, 1993, 207
18. *The Turning Tide*, Pat Robertson, Word Publishing, 1993, 245
19. *A Nation Without a Conscience*, Tim and Beverly LaHaye, Wheaton, Illinois: Tyndale House Publishers, Inc., 1994, 98 (quote from Sproul taken from R. C. Sproul, "A Two-Handed King: Church and State Are Separate, but also under God"), *World*, 22 January 1994, 26
20. *Approaching Hoofbeats*, 141
21. Family News From Dr. James Dobson, James C. Dobson, Ph.D., Focus on the Family, July 1997, 6
22. *The Turning Tide*, Pat Robertson, Dallas, London, Vancouver, Melbourne: Word Publishing, 1993, 271—James Madison, Notes of Debates in the Federal Convention of 1787 (New York: Norton, 1987), 209f.
23. *The Handwriting on the Wall*, David Jeremiah with C.C. Carlson, Word Publishing, 1992, 62; Tyler, Alexander. *Decline and Fall of the Athenian Republic*, 1748-1813. N.p., n.d.
24. *Character & Destiny*, 94
25. *The Things that Matter Most*, Cal Thomas, New York, New York: HarperCollins Publishers, Zondervan, 1994, 1, 218

26. *The Home Invaders*, Donald E. Wildman, Wheaton, Illinois: Victor Books, a division of SP Publications, Inc., 1985, 41-42

Chapter Twelve

1. *The Great Escape*, Charles F. Stanley, Atlanta, Georgia: In Touch Ministries, P.O. Box 7900, 1989, Audio tape-PT279
2. *No More Excuses*, Tony Evans, Wheaton, Illinois: Good News Publishers, Crossway Books, 1996, 314, 315

──── *Signs of Our Times* ────

Signs of Our Times Ministry is dedicated to analyzing world events in the light of the Bible. If you would like to be notified of future publications from this ministry, please complete the request form below and mail to:

        SIGNS OF OUR TIMES
        P.O. Box 555
        Little Rock, Arkansas 72203

[ ] I wish to be notified of any future publications of this ministry.

[ ] Other: _____

Name _____

Address _____

City _____ State _____ Zip Code _____

Phone No. _____ Fax NO. _____

E-Mail _____

──── *About the Author* ────

A former research and development chemist for Johnson & Johnson and petroleum analytical chemist, James Michael "Mike" Hile holds a Bachelor of Science in Zoology and a Bachelor of Arts in Chemistry with a minor in Business Administration from the University of Arkansas. A teacher, speaker, and writer for a weekly Christian publication for several years, Mike is President of *Signs of Our Times,* a Biblically based research ministry. Mike has lived and worked in Little Rock, Arkansas and the surrounding area for over twenty years.

To order additional copies of:

TIMELINE 2000

send $12.95 plus $3.95 shipping and handling to:

Books, Etc.
PO Box 1406
Mukilteo, WA 98275

or have your credit card ready and call:

1 (800) 917-BOOK